The Essentials of World Languages, Grades K–12

PRIORITIES IN PRACTICE SERIES

The Essentials of Mathematics, K–6

The Essentials of Mathematics, Grades 7–12

The Essentials of Science, Grades K–6

The Essentials of Science, Grades 7–12 (November 2007)

The Essentials of Social Studies, Grades K–6 (January 2008)

PRIORITIES
in PRACTICE

The Essentials of World Languages, Grades K–12

Effective Curriculum, Instruction, and Assessment

Janis Jensen
Paul Sandrock
with John Franklin

 Association for Supervision and Curriculum Development • Alexandria, Virginia USA

Association for Supervision and Curriculum Development
1703 N. Beauregard St. • Alexandria, VA 22311-1714 USA
Telephone: 1-800-933-2723 or 1-703-578-9600 • Fax: 1-703-575-5400
Web site: www.ascd.org • E-mail: member@ascd.org
Author guidelines: www.ascd.org/write

About the Authors:
Janis Jensen is world languages coordinator for the New Jersey Department of Education. She previously taught French and Spanish at the elementary, middle, high school, and college levels.

Paul Sandrock is the consultant for world languages education at the Wisconsin Department of Public Instruction in Madison. He previously taught Spanish for 16 years in public middle and high schools.

John Franklin is a managing editor and project manager at ASCD. He has worked as a writer and editor in education journalism for 7 years.

Gene R. Carter, *Executive Director;* Michelle Terry, *Deputy Executive Director, Program Development;* Nancy Modrak, *Director of Publishing;* Julie Houtz, *Director of Book Publishing;* John Franklin, *N&SP Project Manager;* Sara Felice, *Books Project Coordinator;* Nakesha Mincy, *Books Intern;* Gary Bloom, *Director, Design and Production Services;* Georgia Park, *Senior Designer;* Keith Demmons, *Desktop Publishing Specialist;* Sarah Plumb, *Production Specialist*

All Web links and addresses in this book are correct as of the publication date above but may have become inactive or otherwise modified since that time. If you notice a deactivated or changed link, please e-mail books@ascd.org with the words "Link Update" in the subject line. In your message, please specify the Web link, the book title, and the page number on which the link appears.

PAPERBACK ISBN: 978-1-4166-0573-7 **s9/07**
ASCD product no.: 107074

Also available as an e-book through ebrary, netLibrary, and many online booksellers (see Books in Print for the ISBNs).

Quantity discounts for the paperback edition only: 10–49 copies, 10%; 50+ copies, 15%; for 1,000 or more copies, call 800-933-2723, ext. 5634. For desk copies: member@ascd.org.

Library of Congress Cataloging-in-Publication Data
Jensen, Janis, 1947-
  The essentials of world languages, grades K–12 : effective curriculum, instruction, and assessment / Janis Jensen and Paul Sandrock with John Franklin.
    p. cm. -- (Priorities in practice)
  Includes bibliographical references and index.
  ISBN 978-1-4166-0573-7 (pbk. : alk. paper) 1. Language and languages--Study and teaching--United States. I. Sandrock, Paul. II. Franklin, John, 1968- III. Title.

  P57.U7.J46 2007
  418.0071--dc22

                          2007018843

13 12 11 10 09 08 07   1 2 3 4 5 6 7

PRIORITIES *in* PRACTICE

The Essentials of World Languages, Grades K–12

An Overview of the Field

If you don't know foreign languages, you don't know anything about your own.

—*Johann Wolfgang von Goethe*

Thanks to a number of technological advances—ease of travel over vast distances, instantaneous telephone connections, and the Internet—interacting with people from other countries has become commonplace for a great number of us. This unprecedented accessibility to other languages and cultures—whether for social, political, business, governmental, or humanitarian purposes—has created what is now universally referred to as the "global community" and is calling into question our concept of what is "foreign." Our health is affected by conditions and events in China, Africa, South America, and Britain. Sales representatives, bank employees, and computer technicians who provide us with everyday home and business services may be living in other countries. Furthermore, changing demographics worldwide have increased interaction among individuals who speak a variety of languages on a day-to-day basis, in the home community as well as in the workplace.

Time to Reposition World Languages

In this context, the term *foreign language* is a misnomer, and use of the term *foreign* to describe the field of second-language education fails to reflect the interconnectedness of the world's peoples, their languages, and their cultures. The word *foreign* also denotes exclusion, isolation, and alienation, rather than a sense of acceptance, collaboration, and community. Estimates released by the U.S. Census Bureau in June 2004 predicted that Hispanic and Asian populations in the United States will continue to grow at much faster rates than the U.S. population as a whole (Mok, 2004). Hence, the languages and cultures of the world beyond the United States can no longer be considered "foreign." This realization has caused educators in many states to shift their thinking and, as a result, to adopt the term *world languages,* renaming the discipline to reflect a world where peoples and cultures are in a constant state of movement and interaction, and where knowledge of world languages will enable students to think and communicate globally in their future lives as citizens and workers.

In recognition of this era of interconnectedness, this book refers to the languages spoken and taught in the worldwide community as *world languages.* This term is all-encompassing; it appropriately represents the languages and peoples that make up our present multilingual and multicultural global community, but includes the study of classical languages, thereby reflecting the past as well. (Any appearance in this book of the phrase *foreign language* reflects the wording of the source being referenced.)

The renaming of this area of the curriculum may seem largely symbolic, but it reflects a real paradigm shift in thinking about who is studying other languages, when language instruction should take place, what is being studied in language classrooms, and how language instruction is delivered and assessed. It introduces the idea of inclusivity to an area of study previously dominated by the idea of exclusivity. It also underscores the need to create a different mind-set among the U.S. public about the value of language learning to enlist widespread support for the development of well-articulated K–12 second-language programs.

Who Is Studying Other Languages

The adoption of national standards for second-language study was brought about through a collaborative effort of the American Council on the Teaching of Foreign Languages (ACTFL) and other language-specific organizations (National Standards in Foreign Language Education

Project, 1996, 1999). With the advent of the standards movement, the traditional population of students selected to study world languages has changed dramatically. Many states have embraced the national standards document and now acknowledge the value of language study for all students, whether they are college-bound, career-focused, English-language learners, or students with special needs. In past—and even in current—practice, however, college-bound students have made up the greatest percentage of the student population studying a second language. Students in the mainstream middle school population, in particular, have frequently been denied participation because their standardized test scores weren't considered high enough or because of average or below-average past academic performance—perceived indicators of an inability to learn a language. Yet with population demographics changing rapidly in many areas, the need for language skills continues to grow with each passing year.

Moreover, the practice of excluding students directly contradicts the advice given by language acquisition experts, who emphasize several guiding principles in considering language learning for all:

• Language learning is an innate human capability and, as such, cognitive ability should not be a prerequisite for determining whether a student can effectively acquire a second language;

• If a child functions in one language, he is already a viable candidate to function in other languages; and

• Ability to function in the native language expands the student's candidacy as a learner of other languages (De Mado, 1995).

Additionally, educators are realizing that the benefits attained by students through the study of languages extend beyond the practical one of proficiency in a nonnative language to cognitive, academic, and affective benefits—particularly attitudinal benefits, such as respect and appreciation of cultural diversity. The prevailing view of *who* learns another language has therefore shifted from offering language study as an academic pursuit for an elite student population to offering language study as a life skill to be acquired by all students, regardless of their post–high school plans. It incorporates a new world of language learners.

When Language Instruction Should Take Place

When students begin the study of a language is an important factor in ensuring success for all learners. Typically, such study begins during the middle school years, a fact that troubles many language teachers. "It's a shame that many U.S. students do not begin studying a second language before [middle school]," says Rebecca Fox, assistant director of George Mason University's Teaching and Learning Program. "If they start earlier, students have the opportunity to learn a language for a much longer period and to increase their oral and written skills," she says.

Moreover, the practice of starting language instruction late riles many instructors. "We don't wait until 6th grade to start teaching math instruction," says Nancy Rhodes, director of foreign language education at the Center for Applied Linguistics. "Why do we do it for language instruction?" Yet the notion of starting language instruction early sparks considerable debate among educators.

When students begin learning second languages early in high-quality programs, they have time to internalize the sounds of a language, accumulate a bank of vocabulary and phrases, and develop language-learning strategies that will lead to greater language proficiency when they continue language study at the secondary level. Therefore, among educators in the field, the issue of *when* language instruction should take place has evolved from a narrow, prescriptive time frame of two years of instruction at the secondary level to a broader and more flexible time frame that may occur at multiple entry points at the elementary level. "If [students] begin learning before puberty, they will develop better fluency and sound more like a native speaker," Rhodes adds. "But after a certain stage in [brain] development, it becomes much more difficult for synapses to make connections. Starting language instruction earlier clearly has advantages."

How Standards Are Affecting World Language Instruction

The implementation of standards has redefined the content of world language instruction. Standards-driven instruction focuses on meaningful communication and genuine interaction among students through classroom activities that are embedded in authentic, real-life contexts. Most people, when they begin studying another language, assume they will acquire the skills that enable them to communicate with other speakers of that language. After all, communication is the stated goal of language instruction, both in course descriptions and curricula. What was most likely experienced, however, was an emphasis on language lexicon, syntax, morphology, and phonology. Not surprisingly, the learning outcomes reflected the goals of the instruction rather than those of the curriculum: people knew how to conjugate verbs, analyze abstract grammatical structures, and translate sentences and paragraphs with grammatical accuracy using long lists of memorized vocabulary, but very few could communicate at even a basic survival level in the "real" world. "Grammar and vocabulary are certainly important," says Martha Semmer, project specialist with the Center for Applied Linguistics. "But language instruction is more realistic now. We see more emphasis on contextualizing language instruction to make it more meaningful to students."

What should today's students expect to be able to do when studying another language? In standards-driven world language classrooms, students should expect to engage in relevant, age-appropriate communicative tasks that emerge from nonacademic areas of interest and importance as well as from academic content in other curricular areas. The standards guiding the teaching of languages (see Figure 1.1) are summarized as the five Cs (National Standards in Foreign Language Education Project, 1996):

• Communication (exchanging, understanding, and presenting information and ideas)
• Cultures (understanding the products, practices, and perspectives of people who speak the language)
• Connections (acquiring information from other cultures and learning content from other disciplines)
• Comparisons (comparing other languages and cultures to one's own)
• Communities (using language beyond the classroom for lifelong enjoyment and enrichment)

FIGURE 1.1

Standards for Foreign Language Learning

Communication: Communicate in Languages Other Than English

Standard 1.1: Students engage in conversations, provide and obtain information, express feelings and emotions, and exchange opinions.

Standard 1.2: Students understand and interpret written and spoken language on a variety of topics.

Standard 1.3: Students present information, concepts, and ideas to an audience of listeners or readers on a variety of topics.

Cultures: Gain Knowledge and Understanding of Other Cultures

Standard 2.1: Students demonstrate an understanding of the relationship between the practices and perspectives of the culture studied.

Standard 2.2: Students demonstrate an understanding of the relationship between the products and perspectives of the culture studied.

Connections: Connect with Other Disciplines and Acquire Information

Standard 3.1: Students reinforce and further their knowledge of other disciplines through the foreign language.

Standard 3.2: Students acquire information and recognize the distinctive viewpoints that are available only through study of the foreign language and its cultures.

Comparisons: Develop Insight into the Nature of Language and Culture

Standard 4.1: Students demonstrate understanding of the nature of language through comparisons of the language studied and their own.

Standard 4.2: Students demonstrate understanding of the concept of culture through comparisons of the cultures studied and their own.

Communities: Participate in Multilingual Communities at Home and Around the World

Standard 5.1: Students use the language both within and beyond the school setting.

Standard 5.2: Students show evidence of becoming lifelong learners by using the language for personal enjoyment and enrichment.

Source: From *Standards for Foreign Language Learning: Preparing for the 21st Century* (p. 9), by the American Council on the Teaching of Foreign Languages (ACTFL), 1996, Yonkers, NY: ACTFL. Copyright 1996 by Author. Reprinted with permission.

Rather than being the primary focus of study, the second language instead becomes a means for exploring areas of student interest. Content in the grade-level curriculum is learned, reinforced, or enhanced as students acquire and develop second-language skills. For example, 8th grade students in a middle school Spanish class learn Spanish by studying a thematic unit on global warming, concentrating on its potential economic and cultural effects in Spanish-speaking countries. The traditional view of Spanish as a subject area has changed, because Spanish grammar and structure are not the focus of instruction. This is not to say that structure is ignored, but student acquisition of language structures emerges naturally from the communicative tasks and assessments designed around the theme of the unit—in this case, global warming. Shifting the focus from linguistic content to real-world content allows students to use language to obtain information for social purposes, which is critical to acquiring language. This approach also motivates students to communicate and helps students to retain concepts, transfer them across disciplines, and apply them to real-life situations.

How Language Instruction Is Delivered and Assessed

Teaching and learning strategies used in world language classrooms are multifaceted and based on students' active involvement with their own learning. Classrooms once limited to a single text as the primary instructional resource and pencil-and-paper assessments have transformed into classrooms that use the latest technologies to provide culturally authentic materials as the foundation for the creation of meaningful communicative tasks. Students work collaboratively on multistage projects that have a real-world purpose, similar to those they will encounter in the community or the workplace.

New assessments in world language instruction reflect a similar focus and mirror the performance-based instructional activities taking place in the classroom on a daily basis. They allow students to demonstrate what they know and can do, showing their growing language proficiency in multiple ways using real-world tasks. "My students learn how to order from menus," says Janet Glass, an elementary school teacher in North Bergen, New Jersey. "We use authentic menus that I get when I go to Mexico or when I find them online." Students practice ordering foods, sustaining conversations, and understanding news broadcasts in the new language. "We've really gone beyond kill-and-drill," Glass adds.

The culture of testing world languages has, therefore, shifted from reliance on assessing only what students *know* through objective tests to assessing what students can *do* through multiple measures and perspectives. "Because of the broad range of behaviors and functions associated with [second] language proficiency, performance assessment would have to entail a variety of assessment methods in a variety of content [areas]" (Donato, 1998, pp. 169–175). The new testing culture is inextricably connected to a wide range of content and a variety of instructional strategies practiced in K–12 classrooms and, most important, has the primary goal of emphasizing achievement for all learners.

Balancing the Curriculum

The critical need to include the study of world languages in the core curriculum has been consistently reiterated in reports, studies, journals, and articles published within the past several years. The National Association of State Boards of Education (NASBE), in response to the concerns of its members about the status of both arts and world languages study in the United States, examined the current trend in U.S. education policy of narrowing the curriculum to focus on federal and state accountability mandates. Despite this trend, parents and the public at large support a comprehensive education that includes the study of academic areas beyond English language arts and mathematics (Hayward & Siaya, 2001).

The 2003 NASBE report *The Complete Curriculum: Ensuring a Place for the Arts and Foreign Languages in America's Schools* provides a compilation of research on the cognitive and affective benefits of the study of world languages and the advantages of early language learning; presents an overview of the current state of world language education in U.S. schools; and recommends policies to support the inclusion of world language instruction in states' core curricula. Among these recommendations are the following:

1. Adopt high-quality licensure requirements for staff in the arts and foreign languages that are aligned with student standards in these subject areas.

2. Ensure adequate time for high-quality staff development in the arts and foreign languages.

3. Ensure adequate staff expertise at the state agency in the areas of arts and foreign languages.

4. Incorporate both the arts and foreign languages into core graduation requirements, while simultaneously increasing the number of credits for graduation.

5. Encourage higher education institutions to increase standards for admission and include arts and foreign language courses when calculating high school grade point averages.

6. Incorporate arts and foreign language learning into K–12 standards, curriculum frameworks, and course requirements. Also, encourage local school districts to incorporate the arts and foreign languages into instruction in the early years, whenever possible.

7. Advocate continued development of curriculum materials for the arts and foreign languages from the textbook publishing industry.

8. Incorporate all core subject areas, including the arts and foreign languages, into the improvement strategies promoted by No Child Left Behind (NCLB).

9. Urge the National Assessment Governing Board to increase the frequency of administration of the National Assessment of Educational Progress (NAEP) assessments for both the arts and foreign languages.

10. Urge the U.S. Congress and state legislatures to make a greater commitment to the arts and foreign languages (NASBE, 2003, pp. 5–25).

In *Academic Atrophy: The Condition of the Liberal Arts in America's Public Schools*, Claus von Zastrow (2004), senior program director of the

Learning First Alliance, reports on the waning commitment of time and resources for teaching the liberal arts in the United States, especially in schools with high minority populations. The report is based on the results of a survey of 1,000 principals that explored K–12 students' access to a liberal arts curriculum in schools in Illinois, Maryland, New Mexico, and New York. Approximately three-quarters of the principals surveyed reported increases in instructional time for reading, writing, and mathematics—all subject areas for which their schools are held accountable by NCLB. Similar increases were found in professional development for these three areas. A decreased commitment was reported for the arts, foreign languages, and elementary social studies. For foreign languages, both increases (11 percent) and decreases (9 percent) were reported in low-minority schools, but in high-minority schools, 23 percent of the principals reported decreases in foreign language instruction (von Zastrow, 2004, p. 17). Most principals reported that instructional time had decreased greatly, and only 9 percent reported increases in foreign language instruction. In high-minority schools, 29 percent of principals expected further decreases in the future, and half of these expected the decreases to be large. In contrast, in low-minority schools, only 14 percent predicted future declines. The report concluded that "the possibility that minorities are more likely to experience a narrowing of the curriculum raises important questions of educational equity" (2004, p. 9).

"Curriculum for the 21st century must cultivate a variety of potentials and possibilities that are of long-term value, which enrich students in ways aesthetic and interpersonal as well as financial," says Scott Shuler (2003, p. 45), an arts education consultant with the Connecticut Department of Education. The role of world languages in the core curriculum is difficult to dispute when viewed in this context.

As language learners, students take an active role in constructing meaning from their personal experiences, an approach that reflects the philosophy and beliefs of educating the whole child. Moreover, language learning provides students with knowledge and skills across a range of subjects, not just those that are tested.

"The United States must invest in an educational infrastructure that produces knowledge of languages and cultures, and must be able to steadily train a sufficient and diverse pool of American students to meet the needs of government agencies, the private sector, and education itself," says the American Council on Education (2002). "Developing global competence is a long-term undertaking and must begin at an early age, especially for foreign language acquisition" (pp. 7, 10). A curriculum that excludes the study of world languages does not meet the current demands of globalization; it does not prepare our children for the roles they will play as adults and workers in an interdependent world; and it runs the risk of permitting the United States to fall further behind other nations where world language study is more prevalent. In many European nations, for instance, statistics show that 45 percent of people are fluent enough to converse in a second language. In some countries, this rate rises to 80 percent (Wilcox, 2006).

Despite the compelling rationale for the inclusion of world languages as an essential component of the core curriculum by policymakers, educators, and the government and business communities, the appropriate resources to ensure such inclusion are not being allocated. Catharine Keatley (2004), associate director of the National Capital Language Resource Center, reports, "Total funding for foreign language education in the U.S. Department of Education (ED) budget in 2003 was a maximum of $85,425,469, which constitutes 0.15 percent of the overall ED budget. In other words, for each $100 spent by the Department of Education in 2003 . . . 15 cents . . . was spent on foreign language education" (p. 15).

Creating a New Frame for the Value of Language Learning

A 2003 study of how Americans view international education, conducted for the American Forum for Global Education and the Asia Society by the FrameWorks Institute (Bales, 2004, pp. 1–19), yielded some interesting findings. Although the goal of the study was to evaluate current thinking about ways to engage the U.S. public in supporting programs and policies to improve students' international skills, the results of the study are applicable on a broader scale to world languages and other areas. In the study, researchers used a unique perspective on communicating social issues—strategic frame analysis—to assess public thinking.

The study found that the U.S. public views international education as a luxury or a set of skills that can be postponed to postsecondary education, especially in a system of education perceived to be failing at the basics. Researchers also found that the public views the reforms necessary to achieve international education as additive, rather than transformative. "As a monolingual nation, we have very unrealistic expectations of what it requires to learn a language," says Semmer. Clearly, these findings have implications for the study of world languages, especially in light of the general perception that learning languages other than English is not an essential component of the core curriculum and certainly not important enough to be included across the K–12 spectrum.

Rather than invoking national security, international relations, the economy, or lack of student knowledge, educators instead must argue for the study of world languages in a way that reflects a new, more inclusive view of the world, the United States' role in it, and the opportunities such study would provide today's students, researchers suggest. "Americans have this grand illusion that everything that's worth knowing is in English, and that's not the case," Semmer says. "For kids to gain and access the ways of thinking and perspectives of other people is an amazing thing, [and] those kinds of multiple perspectives are going to be necessary to solve the many challenges that the world is facing." Educators and specialists further advise beginning public communications with vivid examples of schools that are making the transformation to international education. They underscore the importance of defining the difference between what currently exists and the vision of what needs to be developed to encompass a global perspective, thereby assigning accountability to the system.

Rather than narrowly addressing current problems, frames that work best inspire a positive vision of what we could become or achieve. Understanding and respect are frames that achieve the most public buy-in. Moreover, these findings are consistent across the entire body of FrameWorks Institute research on public attitudes on international issues both before and after September 11, 2001. As with the Institute's findings regarding the U.S. public's view of international education, this information has obvious implications for the study of world languages and can be of great value in helping educators make their case to the public.

Members of the National Council of State Supervisors for Languages (2002), responsible for implementation of K–12 world languages standards in their respective states, make the case for world languages by reframing the value of language learning for state policymakers in the manner suggested by the FrameWorks Institute research. They have focused on the United States' new role in the world and have created a positive vision of what world language education could be, underscoring the need for understanding and respect of other cultures. They propose several critical steps for educators and policymakers:

1. Advocate 21st century international literacies (i.e., the notion that all children must develop the communication skills necessary in an interconnected world, broadening their view of literacy from reading and writing in one language to understanding, presenting information, and conversing in English and one or more languages other than English).

2. Develop cross-cultural competency by learning languages (i.e., the ability to view the world from the perspective of other people and to comfortably function among people of different cultures).

3. Tap into the valuable language resources in America's ethnic and indigenous communities. Heritage-language learners need to maintain and develop high levels of competency in their first language, and native speakers of English should begin the study of these languages at the elementary level, thereby meeting the need for speakers of languages demanded in the 21st century.

4. Establish a new world language agenda. Improve world language education in the United States through reforms in teacher training, curriculum and assessment, and the use of technology (Sandrock & Wang, 2005, pp. 24–31).

By establishing a new frame for thinking about the value of language learning, and implementing new goals and objectives for language study for all students, we will be able to deliver citizens who are able to communicate and function across linguistic and cultural borders worldwide.

2 Realistic Expectations for Second-Language Proficiency

The best part of human language, properly so called, is derived from reflection on the acts of the mind itself.

—Samuel Taylor Coleridge

In the United States, the field of education has long operated on the belief that two years of language study can produce fluent students, and the public has long accepted this as fact. Internationally, however, this belief has long been known to be false.

Research, standards, and performance guidelines tell a different story, describing what students can be expected to do in the language they are learning at key benchmarks, regardless of the grade in which instruction begins. By emphasizing practical communication rather than grammatical analysis in the language-learning classroom, educators are poised to redefine what a language program should deliver.

Learning a language is a lifelong activity. In schools across the United States, native English speakers are required to take English, math, and science courses from kindergarten through 12th grade. Yet the public, and most students, does not accept that learning another language will take just as long.

Two documents can help classroom teachers set realistic expectations for what students should be able to do at key points in the development of their proficiency in another language: the communication standards from the national standards document and the *ACTFL Performance Guidelines for K–12 Learners* (American Council on the Teaching of Foreign Languages [ACTFL], 1999). The communication standards establish *what* will be taught; the performance guidelines establish *how well* students will use their new language. The latter are just as important as the former, because without clear targets for how students should be able to perform in the new language, teachers either rely on textbooks to set language-learning goals or teach vocabulary and grammar without a conscious focus on the language goals students should be able to demonstrate.

The communication standards emphasize treating language learning as more than simply the development of isolated skills (listening, speaking, reading, and writing), encouraging instructors to operate on the understanding that the kind of language students can be expected to produce will vary depending on its purpose. For example, in an informal conversation between friends, beginning language students will speak with incomplete sentences, occasional mispronunciations, pauses, and the need for the listener to sometimes ask for clarification. To prepare for speaking in a more formal context, however, the same students will take time to organize their thoughts, prepare rough drafts and outlines, revise, and rehearse before presenting a more polished final product. Both forms of speaking are to be expected; it is the purpose behind the communication that helps set a realistic expectation of how well students will use the target language and guides the teacher in establishing what students need to practice in order to succeed.

Rather than having inflexible rules about allowing students to use bilingual dictionaries, work with partners, or memorize material, such decisions are based on the real-world requirements of each type of communication: interpersonal, interpretive, or presentational. Interpersonal conversations, for example, are spontaneous, so using a dictionary would only slow down the communication. Instead, students need to practice making themselves understood even without perfect grammar, exact vocabulary, or complete sentences. "The focus now is on proficiency and language for uses," says Tod Grobey, a German and Spanish teacher in Portland, Oregon. "There's less time spent on grammar unless it leads to an end or has a functional purpose."

When doing a presentational writing task—such as writing a letter to a family abroad that will host a U.S. student on an exchange trip—students attend to accuracy and look up the right vocabulary words to avoid any miscommunication, because the foreign family members are not present to ask questions of the U.S. student. Expectations for designing the task, as well as for the kind of language students will use in the performance, are completely dependent on the type of communication. By designing practice tasks and assessments that are based on these real-world communicative purposes, teachers set realistic expectations as to *how* and *how well* to use the target language.

Does this approach mean that accuracy never matters? On the contrary, experience suggests that students become *more* sophisticated in understanding when it matters. In situations in which the rules of interpersonal communication reign, if accuracy is lacking, it either won't matter because those conversing will still understand each other, or it will impede understanding and they will work it out—asking questions, restating, clarifying, or using other strategies to be understood and to understand.

The second document that has helped to set realistic expectations for student performance is the *ACTFL Performance Guidelines for K–12 Learners* (ACTFL, 1999). (See Appendix.) The motivation for creating these performance guidelines was to put the knowledge gained through oral and written proficiency testing of college-age and adult language learners into a K–12 context. The pathway of increasing proficiency describes the characteristics of language exhibited by K–12 students at three key stages of development, regardless of the age at which they began to learn the language and what manner of instruction was used. The critical contribution of the performance guidelines is to describe what student language looks like in each of the three modes of communication and at each of three developmental stages: novice, intermediate, and preadvanced. These realistic expectations are based on actual student performance, not simply on what teachers hope to achieve or think they achieve with their classes.

The performance guidelines describe six characteristics of language use:

- **Comprehensibility:** How well is the student understood?
- **Comprehension:** How well does the student understand?

- **Language Control:** How accurate is the student's language?
- **Vocabulary:** How extensive and applicable is the student's vocabulary?
- **Cultural Awareness:** How is the student's cultural knowledge reflected in language use?
- **Communication Strategies:** How does the student maintain communication?

The performance guidelines describe student performance for each of these criteria to illustrate realistic expectations for all three types of communication at the novice, intermediate, and preadvanced levels. These descriptions make clear the pathway that students take as they increase their proficiency in the target language.

The nature of each mode of communication (interpersonal, interpretive, and presentational) necessarily affects these six characteristics of the performance guidelines. Novice-level comprehension in the interpersonal mode, for example, relies on gestures and acting out as much as on actual words used to get one's point across. In contrast, novice-level comprehension in the interpretive mode relies on cognates, those words that are very similar in both one's native language and the language being learned.

The performance guidelines help teachers know how much to teach at a particular level by basing their instruction on the way students communicate at that level. For example, cultural awareness in the interpersonal mode would be displayed at a novice level (e.g., as an imitation of the appropriate gestures used when greeting someone); students at a preadvanced level would demonstrate cultural awareness in the interpersonal mode differently (e.g., using the appropriate idioms to express themselves in a given situation, attending to the culture's requirements in formal or informal settings). The teacher of novice-level students need not spend hours teaching idiomatic expressions, because over time students will learn these. Instead, teachers of novice-level students should constantly model the appropriate cultural gestures, knowing that the students will pick them up through observation and repetition. The performance guidelines help teachers set realistic expectations around what should be learned for active use versus what students will learn only for passive recognition.

What are realistic expectations for the time it takes to achieve proficiency at the novice, intermediate, and preadvanced levels? Students with instruction of at least three days per week in elementary grades—beginning in 1st grade and continuing with regular instruction through middle and high school—generally perform at the preadvanced level by 12th grade. Students who begin their study of the language in middle school usually achieve the full characteristics of the intermediate level by 12th grade, while also starting to show characteristics of the preadvanced level. Students who begin their study of language in senior high will begin to reach only the intermediate level by 12th grade. An even stronger argument for starting language instruction in elementary grades is not that students acquire traditional grammatical knowledge but that *they gain greater confidence and flexibility in using the target language*, especially in interpersonal conversation.

Figure 1.1 (see p. 6) provides a glimpse of what the communication standards and performance guidelines look like in the assessments of a standards-based language classroom, compared with more traditional testing of the four isolated skills of listening, speaking, reading, and writing.

Realistic expectations need to guide all instructional decisions. Teachers, parents, and students must base their expectations for successful language learning on the characteristics of real-world communication and accurate descriptions of the stages through which students progress as they develop increasing proficiency. Curricula in world language programs traditionally have been based on a linear grammatical sequence, but the 21st century challenge is to create curricula based on how students actually learn languages and how they will use them.

Reinventing the Instructional Environment

3

To change your language you must change your life.

—*Derek Walcott*

Based on realistic expectations for students' developing proficiency in a second language, educators need to carefully examine the current instructional environment. The role of the teacher changes dramatically with an understanding of language learning standards and second-language acquisition research.

"There is a definite focus now on proficiency and proficiency assessments and language for uses," notes Tod Grobey, a German and Spanish teacher in Portland, Oregon. Rather than presenting a linear sequence of grammar concepts and drilling vocabulary items, standards-based teachers design meaningful experiences in which students learn by using the new language for real communication. In this proficiency-oriented instructional environment, the curriculum focuses on cultural perspectives instead of cultural facts and quaint customs.

The Redefined Role of Content in Language Learning

The content of the world language classroom goes beyond linguistic content and integrates all student learning into instruction that provides a broader range of meaningful, engaging, and authentic language-learning experiences. Content

• Represents important topics and ideas that help students understand the world in which they live and who they are, and

• Helps students respond to important questions that extend learning beyond the classroom (Clementi, 2004).

The community standards encourage teachers to design meaningful learning experiences outside the classroom that may involve multi-step, experiential projects that end in the completion of a real-world task or product. One example of this is the GLOBE (Global Learning and Observation to Benefit the Environment) program. GLOBE is a cooperative effort of schools that is led in the United States by a federal interagency program supported by NASA, the National Science Foundation, and the U.S. State Department, in partnership with colleges and universities, state and local school systems, and nongovernmental organizations. Internationally, GLOBE represents a partnership among the United States and more than 100 other countries, and it provides an excellent means for language teachers to integrate science—and other subjects, such as mathematics, technology, and social studies—into their instruction (Kennedy, 1999; Kennedy & Canney, 2000).

What does the language classroom look like when content is the organizing principle of instruction? Various prototype program models exist for how content can be integrated into language instruction. In the *total immersion* model, time is spent learning subject matter taught in the heritage language, and language learning per se is systematically integrated throughout the curriculum. The *partial immersion* approach differs in that only half the day is conducted in the target language. In *two-way immersion* or *dual language* programs, the student population consists of English-dominant speakers and heritage speakers of a specific language. Subject content and language skills are taught half the time in the heritage language and half in English. In *content-based* instruction, the world language teacher assumes responsibility for teaching certain areas of the grade-level curriculum. In *content-related* or *content-enriched* instruction, one of the most commonly found models in elementary and middle school programs, the world language teacher uses concepts from the general curriculum to enrich language instruction with academic content.

Concepts from content areas such as social studies, mathematics, science, and language arts provide a natural link to language instruction. Social studies topics dealing with the home, family, community, social patterns, and comparative cultures mirror the same topics taught in language programs. Mathematics concepts involving computation, statistics, measurement, and concrete problem solving are easily communicated and transferred in second-language instruction. Hands-on activities conducted in science provide an excellent opportunity for meaningful student interaction in the second language (Curtain & Dahlberg, 2004). Language arts literacy topics also can be integrated into second-language instruction, with the added value of reinforcing literacy skills. Through the study of age-appropriate children's literature, students can identify the main idea and supporting details, search for key vocabulary terms related to a theme, and guess the meaning of unknown words from context. The incorporation of the writing process in the second language strengthens students' ability to organize thoughts and support opinions.

Thematic units or *learning scenarios* are terms currently used to describe extended units of study organized around a particular theme. In addition to incorporating content from other disciplines, extended thematic units

• Incorporate the *Standards for Foreign Language Learning in the 21st Century* (National Standards in Foreign Language Education Project, 1999) by allowing students to develop the interpersonal, interpretive, and presentational modes of communication; compare and contrast the native and target languages and cultures; gather and share information from the point of view of both the native and target cultures; and connect learners to a language community in a real or virtual manner.

• Are of high interest and are age- and level-appropriate.

• Incorporate authentic target language materials and the use of technology.

• Promote the development of critical-thinking skills.

• Involve learners in the development of a final product of their choice, using the target language to conduct research and gain new knowledge about their own and other cultures.

• Allow students to begin to see the purpose of language study as something with real-world value and lifelong advantages. (adapted from Spinelli & Nerenz, 2004, p. 3)

Good thematic teaching captures students' imaginations, is perceived as important to teachers and learners, legitimizes the disciplinary content that is integrated into instruction, accommodates a variety of learning approaches, and has the added value of increased student motivation and an improved attitude toward learning.

And that student motivation makes all the difference, according to educators. "If you start early, you can really get kids' brains wired for learning languages," says Mary Bastiani, world language specialist for the Portland Public Schools in Portland, Oregon. "That makes them better motivated to want to keep learning."

The Redefined Role of Culture in Language Learning

In the prestandards world language classroom, the teaching of culture typically focused on providing students with factual information about various customs, traditions, holidays, artifacts, music, art, or historical events of the language studied. Textbooks addressed culture in sidebar sections of each chapter that contained randomly selected pieces of information on isolated aspects of a given culture. Culture was identified as the "fifth skill" in the hierarchy of skills in the language classroom, which both reinforced the idea that it was not the most important component of language learning and promoted the notion of a natural separation between language and culture. Such a superficial approach illustrates how culture often has been included as an afterthought in the language curriculum, resulting in negligible student learning in this area.

How has the teaching of culture changed since the creation of national standards? A 1999 study of 12,000 high school teachers conducted by the Social Science Education Consortium reports that although world language teachers support the teaching of culture and perceive they are incorporating culture into instruction, this value is not yet reflected in their actual teaching. Since the release of the 1996 standards, an informal electronic survey of members of the National Council of State Supervisors for Languages (2002) shows that the continuous and systematic integration of culture is *sometimes* found in language instruction (Jensen, 2004). Additionally, supervisors *somewhat agree* that one-way transmission of facts still is the most common means of teaching culture in the classroom, indicating that only marginal progress has been made in how culture is taught since the release of the standards.

Unless teachers are provided with the tools to deliver cultural instruction in the language classroom, the teaching of culture will not change. The time has come for the field to refocus on the standards as the foundation of a new vision of cross-cultural education. It is not by accident that culture is infused in all of the standards (Communication, Cultures, Connections, Comparisons, and Communities) and in all topics relating to communication. Within each of these goals, culture dominates as an integral and recurring strand. The continuous, systematic integration of culture is essential to the teaching and learning of languages.

Language and culture are, in reality, one and the same and are mutually dependent. Teaching language *is* teaching culture, and teaching culture *is* teaching language, because communication is the ability to use language in culturally sensitive ways.

To understand how language and culture learning become an everyday occurrence in the world language classroom requires looking at the anthropological approach to conceptualizing culture found in the standards—understanding culture within the context of the *products*, social *practices*, and philosophical *perspectives* of a society. The culture standard in the national standards focuses on how cultural products and practices reflect perspectives (attitudes, values, and beliefs of the culture) as well as how products and practices interact to change perspectives. Based on the premise that language is culture, the modes of communication in the standards provide a natural means to organize the teaching of culture into the curriculum.

The communications standards support the belief that culture is an integral part of all language use and is learned not just by talking about it, but by experiencing it through using the language. For example, in the presentational mode, beginning-level students might reproduce expressive products of the target culture and describe them using simple language; more advanced students might present the results of research showing how expressive products or innovations of the target culture influence the global community. In the interpersonal mode, beginning students might participate in a variety of oral and written activities after listening to or reading age-appropriate, culturally authentic selections, whereas more advanced students might demonstrate and discuss certain observable patterns of behavior and social conventions of the target culture peer group and make comparisons with those in the United States. Moreover, given the direct link between assessment and instruction, these instructional activities become the very authentic performance tasks that enable students to demonstrate their understanding of the products, practices, and perspectives of a culture through the modes of communication.

The Redefined Role of the Teacher in Language Learning

The framework for the teaching and learning of other languages and culture found in the *Standards for Foreign Language Learning* (1996, 1999) has had a profound effect on the role of the teacher. The student standards emphasize the contexts in which communication takes place and require the hiring and retention of teachers with higher levels of competence in language use and cultural knowledge than in the past.

Teachers also must possess new pedagogical knowledge and skills to implement the more challenging performance-based model of language instruction and assessment—a model that requires instructional activities and assessments to provide students with opportunities to use and create personal meaning with language in a wide range of contexts, as encountered in the target culture. "We had one 2nd grade class that studied the rain forest," says Priscilla Russell, supervisor of World Languages and ESL/Bilingual Instruction at the Princeton regional school district in Princeton, New Jersey. "When it came time to study *el bosque tropical* in the regular class, the teacher asked the kids questions [about the forest] and they responded in Spanish because they didn't even think about answering in English. We try to teach all kinds of activities—painters, works of art, food, songs—all kinds of different things to give kids a neat way of learning that's very, very exciting."

In addition, teachers must understand current theories that underline new instructional approaches for diverse learners and have a solid grounding in the use of technology. These requirements represent a dramatic shift from the knowledge and skills needed to meet the goals of the traditional, linguistics-based language classroom and necessitate rethinking teaching approaches to enable students to meet the standards. The good news is that the development of national standards that define the "what" of language learning and the *ACTFL Performance Guidelines for K–12 Learners* (1999) that define the "how well" of language learning, coupled with recent cognitive research, have provided teachers with new tools to foster change. This shift in focus from teaching to learning has brought along exciting and innovative reconceptualizations of how best to help students learn.

Figure 3.1 illustrates the link to many of the key concepts and goals outlined in the national student standards and the effective teaching approaches suggested by NADSFL and Curtain and Dahlberg. Even though *Key Concepts for Success* is geared toward elementary and middle school teaching, the concepts it describes are highly applicable for the secondary level.

In their redefined roles as facilitators in student-centered world language classrooms, teachers are constantly revising and refining teaching strategies, materials, and activities to meet the needs and interests of all students. Teachers empower learners with this flexibility in instruction, enabling all students to attain the goal of communicative-based language instruction—namely, preparing for authentic language use in the real world. The essential question for teachers to consider in their redefined roles in the second-language classroom is this: What opportunities can I provide in my classes to ensure that all students can be successful learners of language and culture? Figure 3.2 provides an example of the communicative approach to world language instruction.

FIGURE 3.1

Comparison of Key Concepts and Goals

Standards for Foreign Language Learning in the 21st Century (National Standards in Foreign Language Education Project, 1999)	Characteristics of Effective Foreign Language Instruction (National Association of District Supervisors of Foreign Languages, 1999)	Key Concepts for Success: Elementary and Middle School Foreign Languages (Curtain & Dahlberg, 2004)
All Students		
• "All children are primed to learn languages, and they will rise to meet expectations when goals are appropriately set and the conditions for learning are designed to foster achievement" (p. 24).	• The teacher sets high expectations for all students and designs assessments and instruction to engage and motivate all learners. • *All* students are guided to use all levels of thinking skills, e.g., they repeat, recognize, and recall as well as apply, create, and predict. • The diverse learning styles of all students are considered in teaching and instructional planning.	• Activities are geared to the young learner's interests, cognitive level, motor skills level, and experiential background. They are designed to appeal to a variety of learning styles, to address multiple intelligences, and to incorporate frequent opportunities for physical activity.
Meaningful Communication		
• "Meaningful language from real contexts becomes the basis for subsequent development of expressive skills" (p. 39). • "It is essential that learners be surrounded with interesting and age-appropriate materials as a basis for acquisition of a new language system in its cultural contexts" (p. 39).	• The teacher and students communicate purposefully in the target language as listeners, speakers, readers, writers, and viewers.	• Learning occurs in meaningful communicative contexts that carry significance for the student. For the young learner, these contexts include social and cultural situations, subject content instruction, and experiences with activities such as art, crafts, sports, and hobbies. • Learners are surrounded by meaningful language, both oral and written, from beginning through advanced stages of language acquisition. • Teachers consistently conduct instruction in the target language with minimal use of the native language. The target language and the native language are kept distinctly separate.

FIGURE 3.1

Comparison of Key Concepts and Goals (*continued*)

Standards for Foreign Language Learning in the 21st Century (National Standards in Foreign Language Education Project, 1999)	Characteristics of Effective Foreign Language Instruction (National Association of District Supervisors of Foreign Languages, 1999)	Key Concepts for Success: Elementary and Middle School Foreign Languages (Curtain & Dahlberg, 2004)
Student-Centered Approach		
• "Active use of language is central to the learning process. [Students] learn by doing, by trying out language, and by modifying it to serve communicative needs" (p. 41). • "Students should be given ample opportunities to explore, develop, and use communication strategies, learning strategies, critical thinking skills, and skills in technology, as well as the appropriate elements of the language system and culture" (p. 32).	• Lessons contain more student activity than teacher activity. This includes student-to-student interactions as well as teacher-to-student interactions. Students work independently, in pairs, and in groups. Students ask and answer questions that they create with the target language. • Students take risks as language learners because the learning environment is positive and supportive. • Students use language-specific learning strategies and are encouraged to assess their own progress.	• Teachers recognize learners as active constructors of meaning rather than passive receivers of vocabulary and information. They scaffold instruction so that learners become increasingly independent in their use of the spoken and written target language. • Learners use their growing awareness of language and language learning strategies to gain increasing independence and self-direction as learners.
Organization of Instruction		
• "Knowledge of a second language and culture combines with the study of other disciplines and shifts the focus from language acquisition to broader learning experiences for the student" (p. 53). • "Students must be given interesting and challenging topics and ideas that they can read about, discuss, or analyze" (p. 35).	• Students and teachers are not text-bound during instructional time. It is obvious that the text is a tool, not the curriculum. • Students and teachers use a variety of print and nonprint materials, including authentic target language resources. • Students and teachers use technology, as available, to facilitate learning and teaching.	• The foreign language program draws from and reinforces the goals of the general curriculum, including across-the-curriculum goals such as cognitive skills development and global education. • Planning is organized around a thematic center and aligned with content and performance standards. Attention is paid to achieving balance among the basic goals of culture, subject content, and language use.

FIGURE 3.1

Comparison of Key Concepts and Goals (*continued*)

Culture	
• "The study of language provides opportunities for students to develop insights into a culture that are available in no other way. In reality, then, the true content of the foreign language course is not the grammar and vocabulary of the language, but the cultures expressed through that language" (pp. 47–48).	• Culture is a natural component of language use in all activities. • Students have positive attitudes toward cultural diversity that are demonstrated in the learning environment.	• Culture is learned through experiences with cultural materials and practices. Elements from the target language's culture are essential components of all planning and teaching.
Standards for Foreign Language Learning in the 21st Century (National Standards in Foreign Language Education Project, 1999)	**Characteristics of Effective Foreign Language Instruction** (National Association of District Supervisors of Foreign Languages, 1999)	**Key Concepts for Success: Elementary and Middle School Foreign Languages** (Curtain & Dahlberg, 2004)
Assessment	
• "Standards preparation is forcing attention to the broader view of second-language study and competence: What should students know and be able to do—and how well?" (p. 15).	• Assessments are ongoing. Students are assessed formally and informally on how well they are able to meet the objectives of the lesson. Continuous self-assessments for students and teachers are encouraged.	• Assessment of learning is frequent, regular, and ongoing in a manner that is consistent with targeted standards, program goals, and teaching strategies.

FIGURE 3.2

The Communicative Approach—An Illustrative Example

Goals: To become communicatively competent, able to use language appropriate for a given social context; to manage the process of negotiating meaning with interlocutors.

Roles: Teacher facilitates students' learning by managing classroom activities, setting up communicative situations. Students are communicators, actively engaged in negotiating meaning.

Teaching and Learning Process: Activities are communicative—they represent an information gap that needs to be filled; speakers have a choice of what to say and how to say it; they receive feedback from the listener that will verify that a purpose has been achieved; authentic materials are used. Students usually work in small groups.

Interaction: Student–Teacher and Student–Student: Teacher initiates interactions between students and sometimes participates. Students interact a great deal with each other in many configurations.

Dealing with Feelings: Emphasis is on developing motivation to learn through establishing meaningful, purposeful things to do with the target language. Individuality is encouraged as well as cooperation with peers, which both contribute to a sense of emotional security with the target language.

View of Language and Culture: Language is for communication. Linguistic competence must be coupled with an ability to convey intended meaning appropriately in different social contexts. Culture is the everyday life of native speakers of the target language. Nonverbal behavior is important.

Aspects of Language the Approach Emphasizes: Functions are emphasized over forms, with simple forms learned for each function before more complex forms. Students work at discourse level. They work on speaking, listening, reading, and writing from the beginning. Consistent focus is placed on negotiated meaning.

Role of Students' Native Language: Students' native language usually plays no role.

Means for Evaluation: Informal evaluation takes place when the teacher advises or communicates; formal evaluation is by means of an integrative test with a real communicative function.

Response to Student Errors: Errors of form are considered natural; students with incomplete knowledge still can succeed as communicators.

Source: From "Eight Approaches to Language Teaching," by G. Doggett, 2003, *CAL Digest Series 1: Complete Collection*, p. 168. Washington, DC: Center for Applied Linguistics. Copyright 2003 by the Center for Applied Linguistics. Reprinted with permission.

4 Designing Curriculum via Assessment Targets

Americans are people who prefer the Continent to their own country, but refuse to learn its languages.

—*Edward Verrall Lucas*

Starting with the benchmarks for developing proficiency in a second language, teachers and supervisors design an effective curriculum by capturing the targeted student performance in unit-level assessments. This backward design is critical to moving language teaching away from the linear sequence of vocabulary and grammar. Using lessons learned from research on second-language acquisition, teachers are better able to design a curriculum that identifies what knowledge and skills students need to do a specific communicative task, rather than listing an entire grammar topic and leaving the teacher to find a meaningful use for it. In addition, students practice these communication skills in a thematic context that is meaningful, engaging, and cognitively challenging. Identifying appropriate measures to assess students' developing proficiency is essential to effective curriculum planning.

Planning Curriculum

Planning curriculum gives teachers an opportunity to look closely at what they are teaching and identify the real goals for their instruction. Teachers reveal the actual curriculum they are teaching when they identify the focus of the day's lesson or their current unit. Comparing a teacher's reflection on what is being taught with the planned or written curriculum gives the teacher, administrator, content supervisor, parent, and student an insight into the true focus of the daily and unit-level planning.

Teachers of languages have been on a curriculum journey for the past 20 years or more, a journey that has dramatically affected how they answer the question "What are you teaching?" In the prestandards world language classroom, many teachers created curriculum simply by writing down the table of contents from the selected textbook. The topics for instruction were a linear sequence of grammar points and topical vocabulary. When asked what they were teaching, world language teachers might respond with the grammar item of the week—such as -ar verbs or *passé composé*—and the vocabulary topic, which might be colors, food, or shopping. With such discrete items as the focus for instruction, the daily lesson plan centered on drills and practice activities to teach the grammar concepts and vocabulary of the unit.

The challenge inherent in using grammar and vocabulary to organize the curriculum is the lack of any indication of how much of each item to teach. How much knowledge of stem-changing verbs do beginning students need? How much drilling of irregular verb forms? How many names for body parts need to be memorized? What names of furniture items should be taught? How much about various structures do students need to know in their first, third, or fifth year of instruction? Without clear goals for students' language performance, teachers designed instruction in which students learned about the target language through a set sequence of grammar topics.

This approach to curriculum planning emphasized the activities of teaching rather than students' acquisition of language, and it had a negative effect not only on students' learning but on parents' perspectives as well, a fact that presents teachers with an obstacle to overcome when encouraging language study. "People think back to when they were in high school, and language study meant memorizing vocabulary words out of a textbook," says Valerie Egan, a French teacher in Gladstone, Oregon. "In the past, that's what you got, but the emphasis has really changed now toward using the language instead of memorizing lists and translations. We want students to be able to have an actual conversation in the language they're studying."

The Impact of Standards

The standards-based mind-set for curriculum planning has had a profound effect on teachers' instructional decisions. The focus has shifted from what the teacher does—building repertoire to teach and test discrete items—to what the students do: building their skills in using a new language. Teachers in the standards era must first identify the end goals of instruction. This clear target then becomes a filter through which the teacher can make the myriad instructional decisions faced every day. Rather than seeking better ways to teach grammar and vocabulary and then assessing students' achievement, teachers in world language classrooms must focus on what and how students actually are learning, frequently checking students' progress toward the targeted performance.

For learning languages, the implication is clear: the curriculum is a spiral, with topics frequently reentering and content regularly revisited. The world language teacher does not merely teach a particular verb form, but the applications of that verb form that students will need to perform the unit's end task. Today's world language teacher will not try to teach all six forms of a verb if that unit's final performance is simply to ask a friend questions and answer for oneself, requiring only the "you" and "I" forms of the verb. The teacher will decide when to teach the remaining forms depending on when, or whether, such information will be needed for an assessment task. The world language teacher will no longer teach grammar and vocabulary simply because they are on a list or in a textbook chapter, but rather will teach exactly what students will need for a purposeful and meaningful performance.

By starting with the actual student performance goal for the unit, the teacher knows how much of the grammar or vocabulary items students need to learn. With this type of curriculum and planning, all instruction works efficiently toward the true end goal of understanding and actually *using* the language.

Lessons from English Language Learners

At about the same time that the performance assessment and standards movements were coming into the consciousness of world language teachers, new waves of immigrant students were arriving in U.S. schools. State education agencies and local school districts quickly mobilized to train the teachers of English for speakers of other languages (ESOL), who were needed to meet these new demands. ESOL teachers faced the urgent need to help students of all ages quickly learn English so they could join their English-speaking classmates in academic subjects. Lacking a common language among students for instruction, these teachers were not able to teach English by explaining its grammatical structures in the students' native languages. ESOL teachers used immersion techniques that provided students with many different ways to comprehend written and spoken messages. These teachers had to use English to teach math, science, social studies, physical education, and art, too. Students proved how well they were learning to use English by completing meaningful assignments in those subject areas, not abstract worksheets manipulating grammatical concepts. These teaching techniques reflected the real-life applications that students faced on a daily basis. "Curriculum has moved from being based on grammar to being based on communication," says Priscilla Russell, supervisor of World Languages and ESL/Bilingual Instruction at the Princeton regional school district in Princeton, New Jersey. "It's very exciting to see."

Teachers of languages other than English also paid attention to this shift. They watched the way ESOL teachers were teaching and how quickly students learned to use their new language. The dramatic results proved to world language teachers that they could trust immersion techniques and reinforced many of their beliefs about language acquisition. These experiences taught language educators to be mindful of when and how students will actually use the target language and to let real-life applications guide instructional decisions and motivate students.

Although many similarities exist between the language learning of immigrant students studying English in the United States and native speakers of English learning other languages, teachers also must be mindful of some differences. For instance, each group learns the new language based on a different need: ESOL students feel intense pressure to master English quickly, including survival, social, and academic language, whereas native English-speaking students are less dependent on acquiring a second language for their future success. Yes, languages will open doors and unlock new possibilities for all students, but most U.S. students won't rely on the language they are studying for survival or academic purposes; instead, it will be useful in their futures for career advantages, for the exchange and acquisition of information, and for the depth of cultural understanding it brings.

If they lack the urgency of ESOL students in learning a second language, U.S. students learning languages other than English in grades K–12 do bring background knowledge from learning in their first language. They know how to learn and read, and can make comparisons with their own language and culture, especially beyond the primary grades. In addition, adolescent students are entering a more analytical phase of their learning and can speed up their acquisition of a second language by understanding how it works, rather than just intuitively coming to conclusions.

The lesson that U.S. educators have learned in teaching English and other languages to students is that *planning curriculum must be based on specific end goals*. Teachers need to create a curriculum that focuses on practical and realistic performance targets. Such targets must consider what students can do with their new language, not what they can say about it. Being realistic in determining what students can do in the target language means that teachers cannot simply assume that students have full control of everything that has been taught; rather, they need to understand the process of language learning, which moves from exposure to the language, to some ability to manipulate grammatical structures, to some spontaneous use of these concepts, and, finally, to full control. The true goal for a unit needs to be stated in terms of the functional use and application of the language learned. When such end goals are clear from the start, they motivate both students and the teacher. The teacher faces clear—and, thus, easier—instructional decisions in her daily and unit planning. She has a learning target to help frame answers to questions such as how much is needed of any specific vocabulary or grammar item or which language functions need to be emphasized. Whereas they previously had no reliable source for making such decisions, teachers now can look to the end performance to guide all instruction and assessment.

Redefining the Thematic Context for Language Learning

If a clearly described performance in the target language is the curriculum goal for each unit of instruction, then what is the context for language learning? This is the next decision to guide a teacher's daily and unit planning.

As previously described, world language teachers have been on a journey toward a more real-world application of the knowledge and skills that students learn in their classrooms. In the traditional language classroom, contexts centered on vocabulary topics as teachers developed units on family, school, housing, pastimes, holidays, and capital cities. In today's learning environment, world language teachers must identify the purpose behind studying such topics. "Today's instruction follows a much more realistic strategy," says Martha Semmer, foreign language education project specialist with the Center for Applied Linguistics. "Teachers use a more natural context [to] make learning a language more meaningful for students. You don't conjugate in real conversation or rattle off a list of vocabulary words. Teachers who haven't moved from the grammar/vocabulary focus are teaching in an era gone by." Conscious of this need for a meaningful context for learning, teachers might now extend their housing unit beyond the names of rooms and furnishings to, perhaps, using Venn diagrams to explore common and unique characteristics of housing in both cultures.

To illustrate this shift in context, consider the traditional unit that focuses on family. Students certainly need to learn the words for various relatives and some descriptive words, but the end goal no longer is simply to pass a spelling quiz on the words for family members or to label a family tree. Instead, the unit's context expands to explore the concept of family and differences within a wider variety of cultures. The unit's activities should be guided by important questions for students to explore, such as:

Do grandparents live with the nuclear family? Do children stay at home or nearby as they reach adulthood? What responsibilities do children have at home in various cultures? The teacher determines the appropriateness of such questions based on the age of the students and their areas of interest. Beginning students, for example, will use simple language to list similarities and differences of families in different cultures. Although students still may do some of the traditional activities, such as labeling a family tree, the end goal is something richer and deeper: helping students to understand *cultural* similarities and differences.

Another common unit at the beginning level of language study is numbers and colors. Numbers and colors are not the end in and of themselves; instead, they are tools to get to a deeper understanding of another topic. A potential application for numbers and colors lies within a unit on the arts as a means of expression. Now numbers and colors are important as tools to talk about works of art. Even at beginning levels, students might start with concrete descriptors such as the number of objects, colors, or emotions they see in the artwork. They then might move on to identify the style, the event, or the cultural phenomenon reflected in the work by offering a simple description of it. Finally, they might use vocabulary and structures to discuss their likes and dislikes regarding works of art while doing a gallery walk in small groups.

This broader context for a thematic unit also includes a cultural overlay on several levels. At its most basic, the cultural overlay reminds the teacher to share the connotations of words that cannot easily be translated from one language to another. For example, the English word *friends* can be translated in French into *copains* and *amis*. However, it is critical to know that *amis* is used to refer to very close friends and *copains* is closer to the English *acquaintances*. The use of each word in its correct cultural connotation might be practiced in the classroom with simulation activities.

The cultural products related to the thematic unit are another consideration. An example might include students using the layout of a city map to explore whether people walk or drive around the community to go shopping or to school and whether public transportation is feasible. In identifying what is common in their community, students learn the valuable lesson that they should not overgeneralize findings but instead consider qualifying information, such as how many people are in a particular category or how something varies at different times or for different ages. Students quickly learn in such cultural explorations to avoid saying "all" and to start saying "some."

From explorations of these factual components of a cultural topic, students also begin to develop an understanding of differences in perspectives among cultures. For example, students will better understand a culture's attitude toward conservation when they relate that attitude to the physical geography or city layout common in that culture. This focus on a theme carries learning far beyond mere vocabulary. Such depth helps teachers design instructional units that will engage and motivate students.

Creating a New Context for Assessment

If world language educators think back to how curriculum and instruction have traditionally been designed, they probably will describe the process of identifying a grammar concept and then searching for a thematic topic within which students would logically use the grammar. Unfortunately, the usual result was simply grammar in a cultural wrapping. For example, if teachers wanted to teach command forms, they might assume that a unit on shopping or travel would give students a chance to practice giving commands as they ask for directions on how to find different stores. But even though students may need commands to give directions, they don't need to learn the grammatical concept of command forms to be successful. Students could more quickly learn as vocabulary items the three or four commands needed for giving directions (turn left/right, go straight ahead for two blocks, etc.). Rather than framing the instructional unit by way of grammatical structure, the unit now is framed by the context of a meaningful and practical application of language, namely, being able to both ask for and provide directions. The assessment likewise takes on a dramatically new form with this realization.

Textbooks in today's world language classrooms play a supportive role in creating a context for assessment and instruction. Texts produced since the release of the national standards include cultural thematic contexts, communicative activities, suggested adaptations for students with special learning needs, and performance tasks. "Textbook publishers have done an excellent job in recent years of making language examples more authentic," says Mary Lynn Redmond, executive secretary of the National Network for Early Language Learning. "You see excerpts from newspapers and magazine articles, there are CDs and videos [with the books]. It's a lot easier to connect the target language and culture now." Textbook company representatives agree that because today's textbooks provide packages with a wide variety of materials and activities, the teacher's role is to carefully select and sequence them to meet local learning objectives. Textbook producers typically encourage teachers to take charge of their instructional planning and remind them not to teach the textbook in a strict sequence from the first page to the last. Text materials provide a guide rather than a strict syllabus.

The teacher's role is to focus the curriculum, assessment, and then instruction by identifying the performance target. Creation of the unit involves identifying activities and experiences along a continuum to develop the desired language performance. Some activities provide exposure to the language element, others supply practice in manipulating the language to achieve increasingly more communicative purposes, and some give students the opportunity to apply the language element in a situation of real communication. The planning process also identifies the skills that are being developed, how these skills will be checked, the support or scaffolding of the language performances along the continuum, and at what point students will be responsible for an independent performance.

Setting Realistic Expectations for Performance

One very important aspect of this planning is keeping in mind realistic expectations for what students can do on their own in the target language. In the old paradigm of a linear sequence of vocabulary and grammar points, teachers expected students to master everything that was taught. Tests contained vocabulary taught earlier in the year and the grammar points from previous years; but the degree to which students will be able to use and apply such knowledge is a function of time. Students may drill and practice object pronouns in isolation and learn to manipulate them in a particular unit, and they may also do well on the focused worksheets and test items that ask them to list the proper forms. When thinking only about this one aspect, students perform fairly well; but in the typical classroom, the teacher becomes frustrated later in the year when students do not use object pronouns properly in paragraph writing. In reality, such drops should be expected because students are only at the beginning round of internalizing the concept; they have not yet reached the stage at which they can independently apply it.

Moreover, learning a concept in isolation does not translate into independent use for life. Students require repeated exposure, repeated practice in manipulation, and repeated reminders to check for a particular form in more open-ended writings. To set expectations for students' performance in assessment, teachers must consider what students will be able to do in the target language with or without help, in controlled or open-ended performances, and with the use of support devices or independently. This understanding helps teachers realistically design appropriate language performances for each unit of instruction and criteria that will describe the type of performance that meets expectations.

World language curriculum design for K–12 must begin with the targeted language performances, realistically set for different learning stages, from beginners to advanced students. To help set such realistic expectations, educators will benefit from a study of the *ACTFL Performance Guidelines for K–12 Learners*, which, as previously noted, helps educators identify the key characteristics of student performance along the pathway of developing language proficiency.

Designing Backward from the Assessment to Instruction

Gathering assessment evidence of these three modes (interpersonal, interpretive, and presentational) reminds teachers and students that all three are needed to function and communicate in real-world situations.

Students who feel they must plan their speaking before opening their mouths will be very hesitant to speak with native speakers in the spontaneous give-and-take of most social conversation. Those students who excel in negotiating conversations need to attend to the higher demands for accuracy of written communication, where misunderstanding is less easily resolved. Balancing both concepts is essential.

The ACTFL led the development of a project to examine how to help classroom teachers evaluate students' language use, both in terms of the three modes of the communication standards and the K–12 performance guidelines. Three end-of-unit assessments form the core of this model of integrated performance assessment: an interpretive assessment task, an interpersonal communication task, and a presentational task. The assessment model was piloted in urban, suburban, and rural school districts in six states, coast to coast. Teachers reflecting on the effect of using this backward design model commented on the change in focus it gave to their teaching—specifically, that they kept the summative performance assessment tasks front and center as they made their daily lesson plans. They felt very confident about how clearly the end-of-unit assessments guided every instructional decision and how they could maximize the use of every minute in the classroom, knowing that each activity was leading directly to the final goal.

The teacher designing an integrated performance assessment for her instructional unit begins by realistically focusing on what she wants her students to do in the target language. From the K–12 performance guidelines, the teacher identifies the characteristics of language usage that form an appropriate target for the unit. Then, from within a meaningful context of rich content, the teacher decides exactly what the students will do to show their improvement in using the language in each of the three modes: interpretive, interpersonal, and presentational. These assessment targets then guide the development of all instruction, as the teacher sorts through the variety of materials, drills, practice activities, pair work, and resources that can support the development of the needed knowledge and skills within that context. Daily decisions are based on frequent monitoring of students' progress, gauging how close students are to demonstrating successful use of the language in each of the three modes.

Models of Performance Assessment for Languages

Integrated Performance Assessment (IPA): The IPA model is designed for individual teacher or school district use as a key component of curriculum design. This approach is reflected in some national assessment models as well. The original performance assessment model for languages is the Oral Proficiency Interview (OPI), developed in 1986 by the ACTFL, which then later developed the IPA. Interviewers go through rigorous training to administer and rate OPIs, making them valid and reliable assessments, but difficult for most classroom teachers to implement. Another challenge of the OPI is that for most K–12 programs, students move through only three benchmark levels: novice, intermediate, and advanced. Unless the elementary language instruction is continuous and regular, students will not make it to the advanced level. The limited increments of the OPI make it an instrument that will not satisfactorily chart student progress from year to year.

Other national assessment tools also have been influenced by the national standards' three modes of communication and the *ACTFL Performance Guidelines for K–12 Learners*. Designed for a variety of purposes, these tools are helpful in understanding the critical role that performance assessment plays in the design of curriculum and units of instruction.

National Assessment of Educational Progress (NAEP): The framework for the foreign language NAEP centered on an assessment of the three modes of communication. The test, which originally was scheduled for administration in 2004 (currently indefinitely postponed by the National Assessment Governing Board), included an assessment of interpretive reading, interpretive listening, presentational writing, and interpersonal conversation. The interpersonal task was administered through a phone call simulating a conversation between the student and a potential sister school. The rating scales were closely aligned with the K–12 performance guidelines' targets of novice, intermediate, and pre-advanced (Kenyon, Farr, Mitchell, & Armengol, 2000).

The *Minnesota Language Proficiency Assessment* (MLPA): The MLPA includes tasks to evaluate students' proficiency in the areas of listening, reading, speaking, and writing. All assessments are given in a context that is sustained over a series of tasks; for example, to apply for an exchange program, students are asked to give basic information about themselves, to describe their family, to explain why they want to visit the target country, and, finally, to raise questions and issues they want to discuss with the potential host family. These tasks gradually increase the complexity and depth of language that students use. This escalation is intentional and is intended to gather enough evidence for determining the students' proficiency levels. The target is to determine whether students are at the intermediate-low level on the ACTFL proficiency scale. Originally designed for placement and admission purposes at the University of Minnesota, the assessment has become a useful tool for high school language teachers when identifying performance targets for their own classroom (Center for Advanced Research on Language Acquisition, 2003).

Standards-Based Measurement of Proficiency (STAMP): STAMP provides online assessment of interpretive reading, speaking, and presentational writing. The assessment benchmarks its ratings to the novice-low through intermediate-mid levels on the ACTFL proficiency scale. Simulated conversational tasks are currently under development. STAMP is a very efficient tool for gathering student assessment data for the use of school districts or states (Language Learning Solutions, 2003).

Developing a Language Portfolio

These individual assessment tools provide a wide variety of useful data; however, no overall system for language assessment exists in the United States. In Europe, the Council of Europe's education framework establishes the goal that all citizens will be trilingual. The Council of Europe asks all European Union countries to begin the study of a first nonnative language in elementary grades, adding a second nonnative language in secondary grades. To keep track of students' progress in learning languages and to capture the variety of ways in which students are acquiring proficiency, the Council of Europe has established *The European Language Portfolio* (Little & Perclova, 2002). In the portfolio, students keep track of all languages in which they have some proficiency. They identify how they have learned the language—for example, as a native language, as a language heard in their home or community, through academic study, through travel to another country, or by other means. Proficiency in each language is charted for listening, speaking, reading, and writing through a variety of descriptive statements. Students identify what they can do in each language in which they have some degree of proficiency. The message is that students develop different degrees of proficiency based on their need or motivation to learn and use a particular language.

Several states now are bringing the idea of language portfolios to their schools. Kentucky, Nebraska, and Indiana, among others, have begun to promote the use of a *LinguaFolio* to help students evaluate their progress toward learning languages (Moeller, Scow, & Van Houten, 2005). Their models ask students to look at a variety of language performances to showcase what they can do in the language. The LinguaFolio encourages students to examine classroom data, select best performances to showcase, and then keep a profile of what and how they have learned. The portfolio allows students to track not only the language(s) they are learning in school but also to get "credit" for a wide variety of learning experiences, such as travel, immersion, Saturday schools, or community learning opportunities. Heritage speakers and users of a language can record what they realistically are able to do with the language, which may range from very informal, conversational language to the more formal, professional, or academic use of language.

Further, several school districts have developed common performance tasks for end-of-semester or end-of-course assessment of students' progress. School districts in Appleton, Wisconsin, and Davenport, Iowa, have designed language tasks that teachers administer at the end of each semester in the sequence of the language program, from middle school grades through senior high capstone courses. The assessments include interpretive, interpersonal, and presentational tasks, creating a profile of students' strengths and areas in need of attention. Teachers rate students' performances through rubrics that are based on the criteria of the K–12 performance guidelines, but are fine-tuned to show year-to-year progress. A powerful benefit is the resulting consensus among teachers on the language goals for courses. These assessments are ready to be reported in a district language portfolio, adding a summative measure of progress to the classroom samples of students' work.

Such language portfolios are currently designed to capture informal or classroom data on language performance but lack a valid and reliable outside measure. Adding a national assessment instrument to the language profile will strengthen the way such a portfolio can be used beyond the individual school. When students' skills can be compared with a national benchmark target, the portfolio also can be used for placement purposes across institutions, especially from high schools to postsecondary institutions. This verifying evidence will help teachers and students know with confidence whether they are on the right path toward developing higher levels of proficiency.

With these assessment systems in place, districts and states would be ready for world languages to join other disciplines as participants in the *Surveys of Enacted Curriculum* (SEC, Council of Chief State School Officers [CCSSO], 2004). SEC, a project of CCSSO, currently involves mathematics, science, and English language arts. SEC provides a process for very closely examining the degree of alignment of state standards, assessment, and classroom instruction. State standards and the assessment instrument are coded to the discipline's specific content and the degree of cognitive demand. The scales and descriptive titles are designed specifically to fit the nature of each discipline. Following the coding of standards and assessments, classroom teachers complete a detailed survey in which they identify the amount of instructional time spent on each element of the discipline's content and the type of cognitive demand required of students. The result allows for either broad or very close examination of how well curriculum (as captured by the standards), assessment, and instruction are aligned. The data are a powerful tool for examining teaching practices.

With the development of a variety of performance assessment measures, policymakers and teachers of world languages are poised to engage in an examination of curriculum, assessment, and instruction. National- or state-level assessments provide the measure for outside verification of classroom evidence. These assessments guide teachers' planning by providing the basis for backward design. The alignment with curriculum occurs when units are based on the same state and national standards as the assessments. The final alignment occurs when teachers examine how closely their classroom instruction leads to success on the assessments. Through this process, the real curriculum is revealed: what is taught, what is tested, and what is learned.

Ensuring Articulation

Assessments should form a solid base of evidence for ensuring articulation. Lists of specific grammar concepts or vocabulary topics will vary even among teachers of the same course at the same school, and students will remember different amounts of each. Moreover, assuming that students will be ready to apply everything that was taught is foolhardy.

Clearly, a broader view of what students have learned is needed. Such a realistic perspective comes through the development of performance targets to guide program and curriculum development. Such performance targets focus on what was learned, not merely what was taught, and, even more accurately, focus on what students can do with what was taught and learned. "A paper test in my class now involves situations," says Tod Grobey, a German and Spanish teacher in Portland, Oregon. "I tell my students, 'Write a letter to someone and tell them about your family and what you like to do in your free time.' It's about having them do something with a purpose rather than simply review 15 to 20 words." Envision how this framework could create different conversations between teachers at the elementary and middle school levels, between teachers at the middle school and senior high levels, and between those at the senior high and postsecondary levels. Instead of the accusatory tone adopted in reference to perceived poor instruction at the previous level—based on, for example, students' inability to conjugate verbs in a particular tense, understand expected vocabulary, or produce specific kanji (Japanese characters)—teachers would base their discussion across institutional levels on actual evidence of what students can do.

The Role of Supervisors and Curriculum Coordinators

5

Things added to things, as statistics, civil history, are inventories. Things used as language are inexhaustibly attractive.

—*Ralph Waldo Emerson*

The role of supervisors and curriculum coordinators must necessarily change to develop this new model of curriculum, assessment, and instruction. A key task for these leaders is to support professional development for the front-line implementers, and this goal is accomplished best through collaboration and support, rather than tightly controlled supervision. Teachers need a forum for learning, experimenting with, and sharing best practices. Supervisors and curriculum coordinators, then, become the agents of change to focus world language programs on the development of students' target language proficiency.

What is the role of the world language supervisor or curriculum coordinator in implementing successful communicative-based world language programs? To answer this question, one must first examine the characteristics of effective programs. World language programs that achieve the vision of the standards manifest, to some degree, all possess the following features (Gilzow & Branaman, 2000):

- Curriculum based on both state and national standards (communicative-based, organized around themes incorporating real-life situations, assessed by a variety of strategies).
- Periodic program evaluation.

• Articulation from the elementary to middle school level and from middle school to high school level.

• Ongoing professional development that is directly focused on student achievement and learning needs.

• Inclusion of students with diverse needs.

• Evidence of well-informed K–12 administrators who are provided with information on what constitutes effective second-language learning and how it benefits students throughout the education continuum.

• Support from parents, teachers, board members, and other members of the community.

• Effective supervisory leadership.

In reviewing these characteristics, the world language supervisor clearly has a key role to play in making each of these factors a reality in the district program. Effective world language supervisors possess a knowledge base in second-language acquisition theory, current instructional methodology and assessment strategies, and the latest research and best practices, both in the field and in the broader educational context.

In addition, these individuals typically bring other leadership qualities to the table. First and foremost, they are passionate and relentless in what they do. For world language supervisors, this passion is critically important, given that they must convince the educational community that achieving competence in a second language happens best in well-articulated programs with appropriate time allocations and effective instructional practices. They also clearly articulate how the goals of second-language learning support learning in other areas of the curriculum, such as the achievement of current national and state literacy goals. These individuals more often than not are visible within the entire school community; are viewed as innovators and collaborators with other curriculum areas; and are active members of local, state, and national organizations devoted to learning and teaching.

According to the National Association of District Supervisors of Foreign Languages (NADSFL, n.d.), to provide a high-quality program that implements the national standards and serves the needs of students, local school districts must have content specialists with subject-specific expertise to facilitate needed change. School districts that depend on generalists to supervise their language programs miss out on the knowledge and ability that world language specialists offer. It is impossible for any one individual to possess the depth of knowledge in every subject area that is necessary for an effective instructional program. Therefore, it behooves each district to have a world language specialist who is knowledgeable about current research and best practice in the field and disseminates that knowledge to others.

Figure 5.1 defines five areas of responsibility for the world language supervisor, as identified by NADSFL: what is taught, how it is taught, what it is taught with, how it is enriched, and how it is explained to others.

FIGURE 5.1

Areas of Responsibility for a World Language Supervisor

What Is Taught: Curriculum Design and Implementation

The supervisor of world languages provides leadership in designing and implementing a world language program (curriculum, assessment, and instruction) that develops real language proficiency in all students, including those with differing learning styles, abilities, and interests.

How It Is Taught: Staff Recruitment and Development

The supervisor of world languages provides professional development and assistance to individual teachers based on current research, trends in world language teaching, and district needs.

What It Is Taught With: Teaching Materials and Equipment

The supervisor of world languages analyzes needs, researches options, and oversees selection of instructional materials, including textbooks, technology, and other resources.

How It Is Enriched: Districtwide Activities

The supervisor of world languages provides leadership in developing and carrying out districtwide world language curricular and extracurricular activities for students.

How It Is Explained to Others: Information and Advocacy

The supervisor of world languages—in the role of liaison among language teachers, administrators, and the community—serves as a resource on effective practices, articulates the language program goals, and provides updates on requirements and legislation.

According to Michael Fullan (2002), well-known author on change research, "Sustainability depends on many leaders—thus, the qualities of leadership must be attainable by many, not just a few" (p. 20). How, then, does the profession build capacity at the supervisory level to cultivate the necessary leadership to implement and sustain reform-based second-language programs? A strategy that has been successful in New Jersey is the formation of a Supervisors of World Languages Regional Roundtables initiative. The roundtables serve as a professional forum for district supervisors of world languages and other administrators responsible for the implementation of world language programs. The goals of the initiative are to

• Assist supervisors with the ongoing design, assessment, and implementation of world language programs;

• Provide professional development for instructional improvement based on cognitive research, second-language acquisition theories, current practices in second-language teaching, and district needs;

• Promote advocacy for the study of world languages;

• Work collaboratively with colleagues in other content areas and professional organizations to facilitate standards-based reform in New Jersey schools; and

• Recognize and cultivate supervisory leadership throughout the state (Jensen, 2002).

Regional roundtable meetings are held in the northern, central, and southern areas of the state four times a year and are hosted by school districts in each respective region. At these meetings, supervisors talk about common problems, discuss problem-solving strategies, and share success stories. The regional roundtables were responsible for creating and implementing a statewide initiative of K–12 model programs and an award process to acknowledge district supervisory leadership. Further, they have influenced the development of state documents and policy by providing feedback to the New Jersey Department of Education during the revision of the world language content standards and establishment of a statewide proficiency level to meet the high school graduation requirement.

The first and last meetings of each school year are statewide, involve supervisors from all regions, and focus on a relevant topic of concern in world language education addressed by a recognized authority on the subject. In addition to these meetings, professional development work-shops, designed specifically for supervisors, are offered at intervals during the course of the year. For example, supervisors have been offered sessions on how to train their staffs in the use of performance-based assessment. These sessions included materials to be used as training tools, sugges-tions on conducting training sessions, participation in troubleshooting discussions related to training, the sharing of training results, and plan-ning for continued training and evaluation of the process.

The supervisors' roundtables can be likened to a professional com-munity of learners who have discovered the power of discussing practice together. Roundtable activities have allowed supervisors to learn about and learn through different perspectives and experience the value of giv-ing and receiving meaningful feedback. They also have enabled super-visors to meet at regular intervals to build knowledge, examine each other's work, and keep abreast of the latest research. Most important, the roundtables have empowered supervisors to take on a new role by actively participating in creating structures to promote change both at the district and state levels.

Another critical component for capacity building is providing ongo-ing support for language teachers. An example is the creation of networks to sustain professional development throughout the year. A trained cadre of presenters might offer a local, informal workshop for language teachers to share teaching strategies. Similarly, a state organization could develop a regional network of study groups facilitated by trained leaders, with expert-provided study guides to assist the facilitator. Also, regional men-tors could provide coaching in the teaching of languages to new teachers in their areas. Such networks might meet in person or virtually through videoconferencing, e-mail list servers, or an online support site. All of the above measures address the need to retain qualified staff.

The redefined role of the world language supervisor in this era of educational reform is to promote collaboration and change, rather than maintain the control, order, and efficiency of the current system (e.g., writing observation reports, scheduling, and ordering materials). A professional learning community, such as the supervisors' roundtables, allows educators to influence or change set practices within and across their respective areas of specialization.

According to Rick Donato, teacher educator and researcher at the University of Pittsburgh, "Leadership emanate[s] from collaborations to understand one's local situation, the various perspectives on critical issues, and the possible futures of fundamental change that potentially improve the lives of teachers, learners, and the profession" (2000, p. 116). Implementing the vision of the standards requires that supervisory leadership move beyond technical management, organization, and information transmission. Leaders for change become learners in real reform situations. To respond to the need for an innovative approach to curriculum development or to provide statewide exemplars of well-articulated, standards-based programs, supervisors need to take on new leadership roles and move beyond the traditional definitions of supervision.

Resources for World Languages Supervisors

What tools are available to assist world language supervisors in their role as instructional leaders in the quest to strengthen teacher competence? One of the most useful tools is current research that supports the criteria for effective professional development for teachers. Sparks (2002) and Diaz-Maggioli (2004) maintain that professional development should be ongoing and embedded in the daily lives of teachers; studies show that benefits gained from one-day how-to workshops are very limited. Unlike the fragmented workshop model, professional learning embedded in the daily work of teachers produces deep understanding, transforms existing ways of thinking, and produces a continuous stream of goal-focused actions that change teacher practice (Sparks, 2004).

Several national documents, such as *Standards for Languages Other Than English*, produced by the National Board for Professional Teaching Standards (NBPTS, 2001), also emphasize the need for continuous professional development tailored to teachers' specific needs. For the world language practitioner, those needs include discussion of language, culture, and pedagogy that calls for a differentiated approach to addressing varying knowledge and skills. For example, teachers need to maintain and update their knowledge of changing patterns in language use and cultural norms in the language they teach and include this knowledge in their instructional decisions (NBPTS, 2001).

Supervisors of world languages play a key role in supporting the professional development of individual teachers. They listen to teachers and assist them with selecting, planning, carrying out, and evaluating professional development opportunities tailored to individual needs. Some examples of site-based, job-embedded approaches that supervisors may consider in discussion with their teachers include peer coaching, teacher study groups, mentoring, professional development portfolios, and action research. Teachers also may participate in school or district networks that strengthen content knowledge and pedagogy using these approaches.

Library of Classroom Practices

One valuable resource for professional development is the 2003 video library entitled *Teaching Foreign Languages K–12* (Annenberg/Corporation for Public Broadcasting, 2003b). The videos can be used for individual or group professional development and showcases unscripted teaching practices and student interactions in a range of classrooms. Lessons reflect standards-based instruction as well as formal and informal assessment practices. The videos provide the foundation for a yearlong (or beyond) professional development module that enables teachers to reflect on their own teaching and try new approaches in the classroom.

Designed to inspire thoughtful discussion and reflection, the videos provide the opportunity to learn from the successful practices of other teachers. The language classrooms shown in this library include Spanish, French, German, Japanese, Italian, Latin, Russian, and Chinese. All classroom videos are subtitled in English and are appropriate for K–12 teachers of any world language. The library includes a 30-minute introduction and 60-minute overviews of the *ACTFL Standards for Foreign Language Learning* and new assessment practices, as well as 27 classroom programs.

Within the half-hour classroom programs, teachers from schools across the country model interpersonal, interpretive, and presentational modes of communication throughout a range of grade and competency levels. Concepts of culture, comparisons, connections to students' lives, and the importance of community also are integrated into the lessons. A Web site and print guide accompany the video programs.

Because high-quality professional development is inextricably linked to what is happening in the classroom, to educational reform, and to best practice, the primary role of the world language supervisor is to act as a catalyst for strengthening teacher competence. Supervisors of world languages are charged with the task of creating structures that will support the learning and teaching process in their school districts. Helene Zimmer-Loew, executive director of the American Association of Teachers of German, makes a distinction between the dos and don'ts of supervisory responsibilities. "They [supervisors] do not work in isolation, do not try to identify problems alone, do not make decisions unilaterally, and do not deal solely with the upper echelons of the school community" (Zimmer-Loew, 2000, p. 173). Rather, they should "support teachers in the use of new materials, instructional methods, and the learning process" (p. 174). Supervisors help teachers develop new ways of thinking about teaching and learning in the classroom and of observing how students are thinking and learning. They provide opportunities for teachers to reflect on and discuss their teaching and assist them in identifying the knowledge and skills necessary to improve their practice and seek new solutions. In doing so, supervisors support teachers in becoming lifelong learners focused on how to improve teaching and learning.

Reflections

Every vital development in language is a development of feeling as well.

—*T. S. Eliot*

The time is right for implementing changes. Economic and social globalization is linking people across linguistic and cultural borders. With this shrinking world in mind, language instruction needs to prepare students for encounters with people from other cultures, both today and in the future, providing them with the skills and knowledge they will need for communicating with and understanding each other more effectively. In the United States, 2005 was designated the Year of Languages, and it marked the beginning of a decade-long emphasis on realizing the vision of languages for all.

The ability to communicate effectively with people across languages and cultures is a critical skill in the 21st century. Many countries in Europe, Asia, and other regions of the world have embraced this belief, and it is reflected in their promotion of language learning and linguistic diversity through state, regional, and national policies. For example, the European Union and its member states have set an overall goal for the teaching of at least two world languages beginning at an early age and have put into motion a variety of initiatives to meet this goal. One such initiative is *A Common European Framework of Reference for Languages*, developed by the Council of Europe in 2001. The framework provides a clear direction for the teaching, learning, and assessing of languages for member states in light of the overall language policy of the Council of Europe and its promotion of multilingualism in response to the continent's linguistic and cultural diversity (Council of Europe, 2001). In Australia, due to recent waves of immigration, societal multilingualism in a variety of European, Asian, and other international languages is being encouraged (Duff, 2004). In fact, in Asia itself more students are studying English than speaking it in the United States (Power, 2005).

In the United States, it is still widely accepted that knowledge of the English language, often considered the *lingua franca* (the dominant language of international business, new technologies, and popular culture), is sufficient. Why has this thinking not changed? In a world of multinationals and of import and export imbalances, Americans have enjoyed a position of advantage. By and large, other countries have come to the United States, invested in U.S. initiatives, sold goods on U.S. terms, and eagerly welcomed "Western" products. This attitude also has been reinforced by geography. The United States spans a good portion of an entire continent, and the only language needed to travel from one end to the other is English. It is no surprise, then, that learning other languages is still perceived as an intellectual exercise, certainly not a necessity, and at best an inconsistent priority depending on the international crisis of the times. Consequently, world language education has not yet been implemented systemically despite the onset of globalization and the current era of education reform.

Will globalization lead to an Americanization of global culture? The likelihood appears remote that the trappings of U.S. society will overtake the strong and vibrant cultures that exist worldwide. Nevertheless, as Thomas Friedman points out in *The Lexus and the Olive Tree,* the undeniable rapid expansion of Western culture and influence does run the risk of wiping out the ecological and cultural diversity that took millions of years to produce (Friedman, 1999). Given the potential disruptions that such rapid development and expansion could entail, learning more about the cultures and languages of the world becomes even more vital if our students are to be prepared to face the world of the 21st century.

Will globalization lead to the global adoption of English? Despite the current dominant role played by the English-speaking world powers, speakers of English represent a very small percentage of the world's population—and this trend will continue, according to population experts (see Figure 6.1). The key question, then, is whether the United States can continue to believe that the world will interact in English, and whether its citizens can continue to deny that knowledge of other languages and cultures is essential. Simply put the answer is no.

FIGURE 6.1

Top Languages Worldwide by Population

The Summer Institute for Linguistics (SIL) Ethnologue Survey (1999) lists the following as the top languages by population (number of native speakers given in parentheses). With the exception of Spanish, the languages most commonly offered in schools are not the most commonly spoken world languages. Almost 7 million students in American public schools are enrolled in foreign language classes in grades 7–12, according to a 2002 survey by the American Council on the Teaching of Foreign Languages. Ninety-two percent of them are studying Spanish, French, and German; only eight percent are studying other languages (National Virtual Translation Center, 2004).

1 Chinese* (1,204,758,787)
2 English (324,637,043)
3 Spanish (322,299,171)
4 Hindi/Urdu (240,892,870)
5 Arabic* (221,145,697)
6 Portuguese (177,457,180)
7 Bengali (171,070,202)
8 Japanese (122,433,899)
9 Russian (117,863,645)
10 German (95,392,978)
11 French* (67,031,618)

*The totals given for Chinese, Arabic, and French include more than one SIL variety.

One initiative undertaken to address the need for language study and language shortfalls in the United States was the June 2004 National Foreign Language Conference held at the University of Maryland and cosponsored by the Department of Defense and the Center for the Advanced Study of Languages. The purpose of the conference was to issue a call to action to move the nation toward a 21st century vision of language proficiency (U.S. Department of Defense, 2004):

> Our vision is a world in which the United States is a stronger global leader through proficiency in foreign languages and understanding of the cultures of the world. These abilities are strengths of our public and private sectors and pillars of our educational system. The government, academic, and private sectors contribute to, and mutually benefit from, these national capabilities. (p. iii)

The conference brought together key representatives from the academic, business, government, and private sectors, all of whom underscored the need for a national plan to create a more language-competent society and deliberated on a course of action to achieve these goals. Conference participants reached consensus that existing language programs, even if appropriately funded and coordinated, are not sufficient. They urged the creation of a systematic and systemic approach to world language education in the United States that would include

• Language instruction that begins in the earliest grades and continues with well-articulated sequences of instruction throughout the educational pipeline.

• Offerings that include languages that are central to global literacy and important for future economic and security needs.

• Maintenance and continued development of heritage-language proficiency to promote biliteracy and enhance opportunities for further achievement.

• A financial commitment to foreign language education at the federal budgetary level and by state legislatures.

• Integration of the teaching of foreign languages into the teaching of reading, writing, and other areas of accountability and the preparation of teachers to effectively do so.

• Incorporation of foreign languages into the accountability system.

• Establishment of standards-driven, reform-based policies for teaching foreign languages and cultures throughout the educational pipeline.

• Recruitment of qualified teachers and enhancement of teacher capacity for teaching excellence through preservice education, professional development, and opportunities for exchange and study abroad.

• Development of policy and legislation to address gaps in national language capacity, taking into account existing sociolinguistic reality, recognizing language rights, and promoting multiculturalism and multilingualism.

• Establishment of a national coordinating entity to develop, organize, and oversee the implementation of a national foreign language strategy that will provide U.S. students with the kinds of instructional programs needed to acquire meaningful levels of language competence (U.S. Department of Defense, 2004).

A Renewed Focus on International Education

In 2001, the National Commission on Asia in the Schools released the report *Asia in the Schools: Preparing Young Americans for Today's Interconnected World*. The report concluded that U.S. students had only rudimentary knowledge of global issues and cultures. In addition, the report emphasized that language instruction did not reflect the realities of the interconnected world of the 21st century—a world that requires individuals to be proficient in current major world languages. Moreover, very few U.S. high school or college students graduate with the level of proficiency needed to interact in a culturally appropriate manner with peoples from other cultures. Subsequent to the release of this report, the Asia Society formed the National Coalition on Asia and International Studies in the Schools. The goal of the coalition is to take actions to address the international knowledge gap in our schools.

One of its major initiatives has been the creation of annual States Institutes to assist states in addressing how to improve students' knowledge of other regions of the world, their languages, and their cultures. At the first States Institute, in 2002, state leaders reached consensus that international knowledge and skills are essential not only for individual states and local communities, but also for the nation as a whole because of the effect on the economy and jobs, human and national security, social and cultural integration, and humanitarian responses to human need (Castaing, 2002, p. 8). Viewed in this way, the acquisition of world languages plays a key role in achieving the goals of international education. Every important issue that is international in scope involves interaction with other cultures, and success depends on the ability of our schools to produce linguistically and culturally proficient speakers of languages other than English. The 2002 report further cites model programs in world languages for higher education, heritage-language speakers, and those using business-language resources and technology. Further, it poses questions for state and local policymakers to consider regarding world language programs. To strengthen world languages on the district level, for example, some questions that supervisors, world language teachers, curriculum coordinators, and policymakers might reflect upon include these:

• What are our goals in teaching world languages? What should they be?

• Do all students have the opportunity to learn a second language, *including* a current major world language?

• What percentage of the student population studies a world language? How many complete a sequence of four or more years of study? How many attain proficiency beyond the intermediate-low level on the *ACTFL Performance Guidelines for K–12 Learners*?

• Are there programs designed specifically for heritage-language speakers? Is technology used in any way to assist with language instruction or as an instructional alternative for the less commonly taught languages?

• What local incentives could be put in place to expand the K–12 study of world languages?

The changes required to close the international knowledge gap are substantial and incorporate reform of the nation's implicit policies and current practices in world language education. The National Coalition on Asia and International Studies in the Schools is working in collaboration with national language organizations and policymakers to achieve these goals. One hopes that these efforts will lead to the development of a national strategy consisting of plans and policies that engage the U.S. public's support for actions that address the significant gaps in national language capabilities—gaps that continue to undermine cross-cultural communication and understanding at home and abroad.

Local Advocacy

The initiatives described above share a common commitment to the development of national language and cultural capabilities and to moving the nation forward in producing globally literate citizens. Teachers and supervisors of world languages can support these efforts at the local level. Many educators may not realize that their actions can affect the way decisions pertaining to world language education are made at the local or state levels. Figure 6.2 offers several strategies that world language teachers and supervisors can use to influence the creation of policies in support of quality second-language education.

FIGURE 6.2

Eight Influential Strategies for World Language Advocacy

1. Stay updated about political issues affecting language education at the local, state, and national levels. Example: Check media outlets, such as Web sites, television coverage, and news reports of educational issues.

2. Prioritize issues that your state world language association should address concerning policy and budget decisions that may affect language education. Example: How will changes in the district boundaries affect the population demographics of your school? How might the allocation of school funds to other program areas or the reduction of overall school funding affect program implementations? Share this information with the relevant stakeholders in your area.

3. Earmark specific points in the decision-making process where advocacy efforts will have the greatest effect along with persons in relevant decision-making positions. Example: Get to know the influential board and community members who are concerned about decisions that will have an impact on maintaining program quality, such as proposed time allocation reductions in an elementary program.

4. Inform all education stakeholders about these issues and your activities through newsletters, alerts, and any other media that reach your constituency. Example: Create a Web site to inform people about issues in your community. Update it frequently to make sure the information remains current.

5. Connect with the media via letters to the editor, op-ed pieces, and radio and TV segments. Example: Invite local media to cover your meetings, activities, and events that showcase what students have learned in the program. Consider writing an op-ed piece for a journal or other publication outlining your position.

6. Form alliances with other organizations and key constituency groups. Example: Work with educators at multiple levels in your community to develop coordinated plans of instruction. Also talk with parent–teacher organizations to share information.

7. Be clear about all aspects of your foreign language budget with "bottom line" justification. Example: Recognize that good programs cost money and be honest about it, but be sure to point out that the benefits for students are immeasurable.

8. Establish and maintain an active network of people who promise to participate in the above activities. Example: Network with friends and colleagues. Assign responsibilities so all aspects of a program are covered and represented. Alumni organizations, blogs, listservs, and online postings can help as well.

Looking Forward

7

*He that traveleth into a country before he hath some entrance
into the language goeth to school and not to travel.*

—Sir Francis Bacon

It is certainly no secret that the instantaneous free flow of information
has changed our world. From the business office to the marketplace to
the classroom, our planet has grown smaller and more connected than
ever before. Today's middle school students, for instance, may someday
find themselves heading overseas offices that only 20 years ago might
have been located in the United States. And as population demographics
shift and companies grow more diverse, the need for language fluency
will only increase.

And this need for fluency means that today's students will need to
communicate in many languages, not just one or two. As more businesses
find themselves competing on a global scale, competitive advantage will
rest with those companies that are best able to bridge the vast differences
between cultures and people, and that bridging will start with being able
to communicate effectively and accurately.

Preparing students for that 21st century business world starts in the
classroom, and teachers will need sound strategies that can overcome
many of the common barriers encountered when implementing world
language programs. This section deals with many—but obviously not
all—of the frequently asked questions (FAQs) that educators often raise
when trying to create a workable language curriculum.

1. How can my district adapt world language instruction to meet the needs of diverse learners?

For our purposes, diverse learners are students whose learning characteristics and styles may require alternative instructional strategies to ensure they have a successful second-language learning experience and to maximize their second-language learning potential. Diverse learners typically meet curricular goals and objectives at varying levels of intensity or degrees of sophistication and according to different timetables; thus, "differentiating the curriculum" refers to adjustments in content, teaching strategies, expectations of student mastery, and scope and sequence.

Diverse learners may be addressed in different categories:

- Students with diverse talents (multiple intelligences)
- Students with high abilities (exceptionally able/gifted)
- Students with disabilities (special education)
- Students who are English language learners (heritage-language learners)

Students with Diverse Talents (Multiple Intelligences)

The importance of varying instructional strategies in the world language classroom is supported by the work of Howard Gardner (1983), who maintains that *each student has a dominant learning style that is a unique combination of the types of intelligences the student possesses.* Most adaptations that meet the needs of varying learning styles are beneficial to all learners and add variety and interest to class activities. In addition, a variety of instructional activities and products may be categorized for each level of thinking based on Bloom's taxonomy (knowledge, comprehension, application, analysis, synthesis, evaluation). By designing a variety of activities that require different levels of thinking, teachers provide appropriate opportunities for diverse students whose intelligences range across the spectrum. Figure 7.1 gives examples of such activities according to their corresponding category of Bloom's taxonomy.

FIGURE 7.1

World Languages and Bloom's Taxonomy

Knowledge/ Comprehension	Application	Analysis	Synthesis	Evaluation
What students will do:	*What students will do:*	*What students will do:*	*What students will do:*	*What students will do:*
• Arrange lines of dialogue.	• Dub cartoons or TV shows.	• Identify elements of a particular literary form.	• Write an alternative ending to a story.	• Prioritize solutions to cultural dilemmas.
• Fill out authentic forms from the target country.	• Command others to perform an activity step by step.	• Analyze the lyrics of popular songs to compare both cultures' perspectives.	• Hypothesize consequences if historical events had ended differently.	• Express and justify opinions on creative products of the culture.
• Listen for sequence.	• Apply a cultural custom to a real-life situation in the target country.	• Compare points of view found in two editorials.	• Write titles for a play, story, or article.	• Give and support opinions about issues.
• Explain the "What? Who? Where? How? Why?"	• Interview classmates about their daily activities.	• Analyze stories, poems, and other authentic materials.	• Write headlines in newspaper style on current issues in the target country.	• Evaluate TV shows, movies, cartoons, articles in the media, or presentations.
• Give a description of scenes from a video presentation.	• Make shopping lists and plan menus for various cultural or social events.	• Analyze a scene in the target culture from a play or TV show.	• Predict future events.	• Write an editorial giving and supporting an opinion.
• Describe pictures from the target country.	• Apply rules of correct cultural protocol while dining in the target country.	• Find evidence to support an opinion.	• Write a diary of an imaginary trip.	• Express the pros and cons of policies.
• Define words.	• Classify words, poems, authentic materials, or genres.	• Compare students' customs with those of the target culture.	• Extend a story.	• Give and support a decision in a mock trial.
• Listen and paraphrase in English a conversation heard in the target language.	• Apply gestures learned to an authentic situation.	• Conduct a survey and analyze the results.	• Hypothesize the reaction to different situations based on cultural beliefs.	• Write to an appropriate official in the target country with suggestions for the resolution of a real-world problem.

continued

FIGURE 7.1

World Languages and Bloom's Taxonomy (*continued*)

Knowledge/ Comprehension	Application	Analysis	Synthesis	Evaluation
What students will do:	*What students will do:*	*What students will do:*	*What students will do:*	*What students will do:*
• Draw a picture from a verbal description of a scene or object in the target culture.	• Apply reading strategies to understand authentic texts.	• Identify the best route to a historic site in the target country. • Play the role of a tourist who bargains for merchandise in the target country.	• Compose a poem, skit, role-play scenario, or advertisement. • Create hypothetical real-world situations found in the target culture. • Create an infomercial.	• Justify a list of sites to visit in the target country. • Read an editorial in a target-country newspaper and send a response. • Evaluate the best Web pages for sources of current events in the target country.

Source: From *Nebraska K–12 Foreign Language Frameworks* (p. 307), 1996, Lincoln, NE: Nebraska Department of Education. Copyright 1996 by the Nebraska Department of Education. Adapted with permission.

For the most part, the world language profession has not been responsive to the second-language needs of students enrolled in vocational-technical programs, many of whom possess strong kinesthetic intelligence. Introductory language courses offered in vocational-technical programs most often do not appeal to these students, whose area of interest is highly focused on their particular program (e.g., culinary arts, auto mechanics, or health-related occupations). However, community colleges across the country are introducing an interesting model for consideration; they are beginning to change language course offerings to meet the needs of police officers, firefighters, health workers, and those in service professions who require job-specific language or needs-based language to assist them (Gifford, 2004). Such programs, referred to as *occupational language programs,* include cross-cultural training designed to eliminate misunderstandings that arise in the workplace between English-dominant speakers and speakers of languages other than English. Instructors use nontraditional learning strategies, with a focus on comprehension and oral production of a limited repertoire of conversational words and phrases. At the secondary level, as well, this model may be of particular interest for students who are not motivated to study intensely a second language that holds little academic interest for them. Because the primary goal of these programs is to equip learners to perform routine job functions in the target language—thereby providing an immediate application of what is being studied—motivation to learn a language is strong and viewed as a practical skill for the workplace.

Students with High Abilities (Exceptionally Able/Gifted)

Of all of the groups of diverse learners, exceptionally able learners often are among the most underserved in the world language classroom, particularly at beginning levels of instruction. Exceptionally able students often demonstrate a high degree of intellectual, creative, or artistic ability and can grasp concepts rapidly or intuitively. Just as in other content areas, these students may need accommodations or special instruction to achieve at levels commensurate with their abilities. Once properly identified, exceptional students should be provided with appropriate instructional accommodations that are integrated into world language instruction at all levels. Figure 7.2 provides examples of specific adaptation strategies for the world language classroom.

Students with Disabilities (Special Education)

Adaptations enable students with disabilities to maximize their strengths and compensate for their learning differences. Certain adaptations structure students' learning in a more explicit, systematic way, whereas others provide alternative means for students to acquire or demonstrate their knowledge. Most adaptations used in the world language classroom are based on effective instructional practices that benefit all students, but are essential for a student with disabilities. Students with disabilities often require adaptations that fall into four categories:

instructional preparation, instructional prompts, instructional application, and instructional monitoring.

Instructional preparation refers to how information is structured and organized. Examples of instructional preparation techniques include preteaching vocabulary (meaning and pronunciation); using visual demonstrations, illustrations, and models; presenting mini-lessons;

FIGURE 7.2

Suggested Adaptation Strategies for Exceptionally Able and Gifted Learners in the World Language Classroom

Student adaptations may include, but are not limited to, the following:

• Researching and discussing cultural issues or perspectives in more depth.

• Posing questions that involve inferencing and focus on complex cross-curricular themes or global problems.

• Explaining reasons for taking a certain position or making a specific decision, both orally and in writing in the target language.

• Creating original songs, stories, short plays, poems, and designs that show multicultural perspectives of a specific theme or have a futuristic twist.

• Being held accountable for additional authentic interpretive listening tasks.

• Creating experiences and performances that reflect the results of research, interviews, or surveys in the target language.

• Retelling a story or experience from other content areas in the target language.

• Writing editorials and letters to target-language newspapers in the United States.

• E-mailing articles, commentaries, or reviews to target-culture schools, publications, organizations, newspapers, or magazines.

• Handling assignments involving more sophisticated computer research and reporting in the target language.

• Interpreting assignments such as handouts or information for Web searches in the target language.

• Processing a greater volume of any given print material.

• Independently choosing world language projects.

Source: From *New Jersey World Languages Curriculum Framework* (p. 218), 1999, Trenton, NJ: New Jersey Department of Education. Copyright 1999 by the New Jersey Department of Education. Reprinted with permission.

using brainstorming and webbing; and relating to personal experiences. *Instructional prompts* activate recall, generate classification, cue associations and connections, and highlight and clarify essential concepts. Examples of instructional prompts include graphic and semantic organizers, mnemonic devices, movement cues, manipulatives, and scaffolding. The purpose of *instructional application* is to simplify abstract concepts and provide concrete examples, build connections and associations, engage multiple modalities, and relate to everyday experiences. Examples include hands-on activities; dramatization, music, or movement; drawing or painting; games; and structured dialogue. *Instructional monitoring* techniques provide for continuous checks for understanding, promote participation, provide reinforcement and feedback, and develop self-questioning and self-regulation. Examples of these techniques are vocabulary journals, portfolios, peer reviews, self-monitoring checklists, and student think-alouds.

Students with disabilities also may require specific adaptations for instructional groupings (peer partners and buddy systems), an instructional support person, special seating arrangements, and adaptive equipment and materials. In terms of assessment, these students need to be provided with a wide range of tasks to demonstrate their knowledge and skills, some of which may require extended time and a preferred response mode (e.g., illustrated, modeled, oral). Grading practices also may need to be modified (e.g., use of a student portfolio that shows mastery of certain skills and progress over the continuum, rather than letter grades).

Although some students with disabilities are eager to engage in various world language activities, others are not; this reluctance may be due to a variety of factors, some of which may be related to their individual disabilities. Motivational strategies therefore become important tools to assist students in becoming successfully involved in world language activities. Such strategies include a choice of activities; hands-on, multimodal activities; doable learner tasks; modification of activities to meet different learning styles; student involvement in goal-setting and assessment activities; and the option of working with others or alone. Figure 7.3 provides

FIGURE 7.3

Considerations for Meeting Specific Learning Needs in Skill and Instructional Areas

To ensure success with speaking . . .

• Give sentence starters. • Use graphic organizers to organize ideas and relationships. • Use visuals. • Allow extra response time for processing. • Use cues and prompts to help the student know when to speak.	• Use partners. • Phrase questions with choices embedded in them. • Use choral reading or speaking. • Use rhythm or music. • Allow practice opportunities for speaking. • Practice role-playing activities.

To ensure success with reading . . .

• Use prereading and postreading activities to preteach or reinforce main ideas. • Use specific strategies before, during, and after reading. For example, use preview questions before, pausing to reflect during, self-evaluation and summary after. • Provide advance organizers when showing videos. • Use peer tutoring. • Provide audiotaped materials (text or study guides). • Teach self-questioning. • Paraphrase key points or have students paraphrase key points. • Summarize key points or have students summarize key points.	• Label main ideas. • Label the 5 Ws—Who? What? When? Where? Why? Allow highlighting of texts, passages, key words, or concepts. • Use visual imagery. • Explain idioms that appear in reading passages. • Allow silent prereading. • Allow partner reading. • Use computer programs or games. • Allow students to quietly read aloud (subvocalization). • Use graphic organizers. • Use preparatory set (i.e., talk through what a reading passage is about using new vocabulary and concepts).

To ensure success with writing . . .

- Shorten writing assignments.
- Require lists instead of sentences.
- Allow students to dictate ideas to peers.
- Provide note takers.
- Allow students to use a tape recorder to dictate writing.
- Allow visual representation of ideas.
- Provide a fill-in-the-blank form for note taking.
- Allow students to use a computer for outlining, word processing, spelling, and grammar checks.
- Provide a structure for the writing.
- Allow collaborative writing.

- Provide a model of the writing.
- Allow use of different writing utensils and paper.
- Use a flow chart for organizing ideas before the student writes.
- Brainstorm a bank of possible words that might be needed prior to the writing activity.
- Narrow the choice of topics.
- Grade on the basis of content; do not penalize for errors in mechanics and grammar.
- Allow options with a manuscript, such as cursive or keyboarding.
- Allow different positions or surfaces for writing.

To ensure success with assessment . . .

- Use a variety of authentic assessments.
- Establish criteria and expectations prior to instruction.
- Teach test-taking strategies.
- Teach the format of an upcoming test.
- Allow adequate time for test taking.
- Allow paper-and-pencil tests to be taken in a different space.

- Allow a variety of ways to respond (e.g., orally, pictorially, tape recordings).
- Give choices.
- Assess learning continuously over time, not just at the end of a unit of study.
- Use rubrics.
- Use self-assessment tools.

To ensure success when working in groups . . .

- Teach group rules and expectations.
- Teach skills of independence (e.g., bridging phrases, disagreeing agreeably, voice level).
- Teach manageable strategies for moving in and out of groups within the classroom setting.
- Post rules and expectations.
- Give adequate time, but not "fooling around" time.
- Be in close proximity to groups as they work.
- Teach students to self-monitor group progress.

- Assign student roles or responsibilities in the group.
- Teach a signal for getting the attention of all groups.
- Practice and assess students' behaviors in small-group settings.
- Use cooperative learning strategies.
- Use a wide variety of groupings (e.g., flexible, cluster, skill).

Source: From *Nebraska K–12 Foreign Language Frameworks* (pp. 302–305), 1996, Lincoln, NE: Nebraska Department of Education. Copyright 1996 by the Nebraska Department of Education. Adapted with permission.

concrete examples of strategies for meeting specific learning needs in skill and instructional areas.

Students Who Are English Language Learners (Heritage-Language Learners)

Students who arrive in classrooms with diverse levels of English-language proficiency should be given the same opportunity as others to learn world languages. In the best-case scenario, they should be helped to maintain and develop native language skills and also to study another world language in addition to English at some point in their schooling. A relatively new term—heritage-language learners—is used in practice to describe students with varying levels of native-language proficiency. According to Guadalupe Valdes, Stanford University professor and recognized expert on heritage-language learners, a heritage-language learner is "a language student who is raised in a home where a non-English language is spoken, who speaks or at least understands the language, and who is to some degree bilingual in that language and in English" (2001, p. 38).

When referring to students who match this description, schools have used terms such as English as a second language (ESL) students, bilingual education (BE) students, limited English proficient (LEP) students, or English language learners (ELL). These students may be able to understand spoken language but unable to speak beyond words and phrases. Others can speak the language fluently but cannot express themselves in writing. Some can understand and speak the language well but have limited reading and writing skills due to lack of a formal education in their native countries. Finally, there are those students who can function at a high level in all language skill areas.

What implication does this diverse population of heritage-language students have for world language instruction? Simply stated, *world language teachers need to know and understand their students in order to meet their varying learning needs.* In addition to students' linguistic capabilities, teachers need to have information about students' background and interests to tap into their talents and skills. This goal goes beyond having heritage-language students participating in advanced placement language courses. The ultimate goal of instruction for these students should be to speak and write effectively in an occupational or professional setting. Moreover, individuals with high levels of proficiency in a heritage language are in great demand by the academic, business, private, and government sectors.

Teachers often have difficulty working with heritage-language students in world language classes with monolingual students. This issue is addressed by various experts in *Spanish for Native Speakers,* part of a professional development series produced by the American Association of Teachers of Spanish and Portuguese. The essence of this response seems appropriate for any language class with heritage and English-dominant students and is not applicable only to Spanish. "Ideally, mixed classes should not exist because they are pedagogically unsound. Heritage speakers of Spanish should be in SNS (Spanish for Native Speakers) courses that address their specific needs" (Samaniego & Pino, 2000, p. 32). Samaniego and Pino acknowledge that courses for native speakers are rare for a variety of reasons and advise teachers to challenge these students from the first day of class so they will not lose their motivation to study the language.

> Motivational needs of heritage speakers are very similar to the needs of all foreign language learners. For example, students get bored very quickly if the material is too advanced or too easy, if the material is not relevant to their daily life, if there is too much direct error correction, and so forth. It is not at all surprising that native speakers have shown little motivation in the past in classes where the texts used were designed for monolingual students, did not address any of the heritage speakers' linguistic needs, and where these students were constantly being put down for not showing interest in subject matter far too simplistic for their linguistic levels. Therefore, to motivate these students, it is important that the course content address the linguistic needs of the students and provide appropriate cultural and literary readings. Teachers must always respect the language heritage speakers bring to the class, putting emphasis on alternative ways of saying things rather than insisting on eliminating community and family language patterns. (2002, p. 36)

The following are some additional options for heritage-language students when considering the study of a world language:

Study of a world language other than English and other than the heritage language. Students may elect to study any world language in addition to English offered in the school district's world language program.

Further study of the heritage language. Students may continue to develop and enhance their native language in either a program designed specifically for native speakers of a particular language or in an out-of-school program if that language is not taught in the public school district. For example, in New Jersey, legislation requires that the Department of Education establish a World Languages Instruction Committee to develop a plan that allows students in public schools to receive instruction in, and graduation credit for, a world language not taught in the district. In compliance with this law, the department established a committee that has developed an implementation plan to be followed by districts, upon the written request of a student and that student's parent(s), which grants graduation credit for a language program offered by an external organization. An external organization is defined as a nonprofit organization such as a church or community group. The committee also has developed procedures for external organizations that seek district approval for their world languages programs. These procedures provide a uniform template that districts and external organizations follow to ensure credit is properly awarded to students (New Jersey Department of Education, 2004).

Satisfy requirements with the heritage language. Students may use their native language to satisfy a district or state high school language requirement when entering the 9th grade or at subsequent grade levels as newly arrived students from their native countries. Many, but not all, students who have been speaking, reading, and writing in their native language since a very young age and throughout their prior educational experience may have high proficiency levels in their native language that will satisfy requirements. This ability can be documented with proficiency testing.

2. How can my school or district find qualified world language teachers?

To deliver the kind of instruction that helps students develop true proficiency in using the target language, a teacher needs to have a high degree of skill in using the language, regardless of the level being taught. The language teacher at the beginning level(s)—whether the program begins in the elementary grades, middle school grades, or senior high—sets an expectation for students regarding the nature of learning a language. If the experience is mainly one of talking about the language in English or is simply a program meant to teach some words and cultural holidays, students will not acquire useful language-learning habits. At the beginning level, students will learn the new language better if they use it to learn important content. A balance of communication modes is also critical, so that students don't come to expect that language classes will focus only on listening and speaking. "We need qualified teachers [who have] both the language background and adequate pedagogical skills," says Martha Semmer, foreign language education project specialist with the Center for Applied Linguistics (CAL). "The only way foreign language programs fly is if they have a strong connection to the curriculum." Teachers must help students who already have literacy skills in their first language to tap into those skills in learning other languages.

Policymakers wanting to encourage this type of language-learning experience need to establish a state or district minimum standard for the oral proficiency of any language teacher. Several state education agencies have set a minimum standard for that oral proficiency. Such states have selected a benchmark from the oral proficiency guidelines established by ACTFL, targeting either the intermediate-high or advanced-low level for initial certification. The National Council for the Accreditation of Teacher Education (NCATE) has identified advanced-low as the minimum oral proficiency to require of future language teachers. Many states also require a period of immersion in the culture through time spent studying, living, or working abroad. This immersion requirement could also be met through domestic experiences, using the target language to a degree similar to that needed when living abroad by interacting with native speakers of the language. Such immersion requirements provide the prospective teacher with first-hand knowledge of the target culture as well as the confidence of having success in fully interacting with native speakers.

Recruiting Highly Qualified Language Teachers

Having established this necessary standard for language instructors, school administrators are tasked with finding such highly qualified teachers. Recruitment efforts are not solely the realm of administrators; professional organizations also need to get involved.

Recruiting students from high school and university programs. Professional organizations, such as those serving language teachers or directors of instruction, have become proactive in bringing potential teachers into the activities of their organizations. Numerous state organizations of world language teachers have set up programs in which high school language teachers bring students to their state conventions. To provide role models and create interest in considering language teaching as a career, convention planners have organized special workshops for the guest high school students, where recently graduated teachers share their language learning experiences and tell why and how they became language teachers. Special recognition events welcome the high school students into the profession. For university students, several state language teachers' organizations provide scholarships to subsidize the cost of attending their state conventions and again provide special workshops or events to answer the questions of these future teachers, as well as begin a network for ongoing support as they go through student teaching or first years of employment.

Recruiting from an international pool. Several state education agencies have entered into memoranda of understanding with the education offices of foreign embassies, with the prime goal of encouraging foreign teachers to serve as language teachers in the state. Whether arranged through a third party, such as Visiting International Faculty, Inc., or through the state education agency, these efforts have resulted in hundreds of foreign teachers helping to relieve the shortage of language teachers in certain states. Texas employs more than 300 foreign teachers to fill such vacancies; North Carolina employs more than 50. These efforts are not meant to replace U.S. citizens in these positions, but are helpful to districts that have been unable to fill certain language teaching jobs. The teacher from abroad brings native language and culture to the school and also benefits the nonnative-speaking language teachers in the district. The foreign teachers and the U.S. teachers learn from one another; the foreign teachers share their language and culture, and the U.S. teachers share teaching strategies that are successful in U.S. schools.

Recruiting heritage speakers. Heritage speakers are people already in the United States with some proficiency in the language of their heritage; however, the proficiency may range from very limited understanding of what is heard to highly developed writing and speaking skills. For example, a person who has grown up in the United States in a household where grandparents speak a language other than English may be able to understand them but be unable to respond in that language and possess virtually no literacy skills. Such heritage speakers possess a rich cultural tradition but need to develop their language skills. Other heritage speakers may be quite bilingual, somewhere along a continuum ranging from informal usage only to application in a wide variety of professional and academic settings.

Heritage speakers might be recruited through scholarships from community or heritage organizations, because these groups have a direct interest in maintaining their language and culture. Some state organizations serving the needs of recent immigrants, for example, have provided scholarships and encouragement for young adults to enter teacher training programs to obtain employment as bilingual teaching aides, bilingual classroom teachers, or language teachers to mainly native English speakers. Such efforts provide incentives for heritage students to serve the language needs of the local language community by becoming educators, assisting other heritage speakers and students. This is one way to help provide a supply of teachers for the less commonly taught languages in schools, such as Japanese, Italian, Hebrew, Arabic, and American Sign Language. Heritage speakers possess language skills and cultural knowledge upon which they can build as they prepare to teach the language of their heritage.

With such prior knowledge and skill, these future teachers begin at a more advanced level in their language training and can thus concentrate more quickly on the specific strategies needed to teach languages. Such a valuable resource must be tapped to increase the number of U.S. schools offering Arabic, Chinese, Indonesian, and other non-European languages.

3. Why is it important to demonstrate student proficiency in the elementary grades, middle school, and senior high programs?

Very few states require any assessment of world languages. State education agencies may provide assistance with the design of world language assessments or sample assessments but not the type of assessment that currently directs program design in the tested areas of English language arts and reading, social studies, science, and mathematics. Without state assessment of students' skills and knowledge in languages other than English, local districts need to prove the value of their programs with appropriate evidence. Such evidence should capture language performances in terms that the public expects and accepts—that is, evidence showing real-world application of the language. Assessments should provide evidence of how well students hold conversations with native speakers, understand the gist of written and spoken messages, and present information in ways that are linguistically and culturally appropriate.

Districts that are consciously addressing these issues of assessment will be ready to respond when different groups ask for a justification of their program(s). This question will come from a variety of sources: the middle school language teacher will ask it of the elementary language teacher; the senior high language teacher will ask it of the middle school teacher; university faculty in charge of language placement will ask for such evidence from the senior high staff; school boards will ask administrators to show how effective the program is; the public will want evidence of what students are actually learning as a result of their investment in the program; and parents and students will need proof that students have learned something of practical value. By providing assessments that fit these demands—not tests on grammar and vocabulary but assessments showing real language applications—teachers and administrators will help all of these groups understand the true goals of the program. Assessments of this nature make a very positive statement about the skills being developed in students, and measurable proof of achievement will help language programs survive in tough budget times.

4. Where can I find adequate resources to implement an effective program?

Instructional Materials

Thanks to technology, the wealth of powerful and affordable resources now available to teachers of world languages is almost immeasurable. For example, the use of Internet materials minimizes the costs incurred in purchasing textbooks for all students and is a pedagogically sound alternative. Online technologies enable students to access up-to-the-minute, authentic cultural materials and realia. E-mail, electronic conferencing, and online performance assessments are only a few of the many instructional tools available that provide a means for real-life communication. Audio and video segments that illustrate a wide variety of speakers of a given language provide access to many speaking styles, voices, and accents while providing a realistic look at the target culture that is not possible through conventional means.

In addition, by the very nature of the profession, world language teachers are fortunate in being able to obtain instructional materials through various embassies and consulates that represent the language and culture being taught, heritage-language community resources, and international exchanges and trips. Teachers also have access to resources available through other means, such as language-specific organizations, electronic mailing lists, or workshops and conferences.

Curriculum Development

The New Visions in Action (NVIA) Project, a national grant-funded initiative, seeks to revamp the language education system so that it can achieve the important goal of language proficiency for all students. The goal of the Curriculum, Instruction, Assessment, and Articulation Task Force of the NVIA Project is to produce online and paper documents that synthesize information for guiding and informing local decision making in the areas of curriculum, instruction, assessment, and articulation. The information obtained from this project is available online at no cost to educators at www.educ.iastate.edu/newvisions and represents a reliable source to inform work done in these areas.

Information on curriculum development and related topics also is available on the Web sites of most states and through the National Foreign Language Resource Centers, funded by grants from the U.S. Department of Education. The mission of these centers is to improve the teaching and learning of foreign languages in the United States; 15 centers exist nationwide, and each has a different focus (see the Resources section of this book). For example, the National K–12 Foreign Language Resource Center at Iowa State University focuses solely on the improvement of student learning of foreign languages at the elementary and secondary school levels. The center conducts research, develops publications, and holds summer institutes for teachers that revolve around the themes of curriculum development, innovative technology, performance assessment, action research, foreign language student standards, and professional collaboration. Past projects include the creation of a guide to assist teachers in aligning their present foreign language curriculum with the national standards for student learning. The document enables teachers to identify what aspects of their current curriculum fit with the standards and how these can be extended and adapted to address the new dimensions of the standards. The center also has created thematic units to assist with content-related teaching at the elementary level.

5. How do I apply the vision of standards-based language instruction in my classroom? Where do I begin?

One way to begin the transition from a traditional textbook approach to a standards-driven approach to language learning is by doing an honest self-assessment of your teaching. The following questions and prompts are designed to be considered in discussions about your district language program with your colleagues or staff. They were compiled by New Jersey supervisors of world languages for the purpose of evaluation and may be duplicated for educational purposes. After discussing the questions, you and your colleagues or staff may wish to consider (1) new ideas or questions raised by this book and (2) actions you intend to take in response.

1. Are ongoing professional development opportunities available for the world language staff, both in-district and out-of-district?

2. Do world language teachers have common planning time available for curriculum development? Is planning time provided to foster curriculum integration with other content-area teachers?

3. Describe the assessment philosophy and types of assessments used in the world languages program.

4. How does the school district provide for both vertical and horizontal articulation among schools in the district?

5. How are students grouped for world language instruction? How are needs met for the special education population? For heritage-language learners?

6. How are world languages scheduled in the school day at the elementary and middle school levels?

7. To what degree do the school administration, the board of education, and the community support the world language program?

8. Describe any areas that need improvement in your program.

9. Identify the strongest components of your program.

Resources

Organizations

American Council on the Teaching of Foreign Languages (ACTFL)
www.actfl.org

ACTFL's mission is to provide vision, leadership, and support for quality teaching and learning of languages. From the development of proficiency guidelines to a leadership role in the creation of national and language-specific standards, from representation for languages in cross-curricular initiatives to the implementation of innovations in teacher training, ACTFL focuses on issues that are critical to the growth of the profession and the individual teacher.

The links provided through the ACTFL Web site are current and comprehensive in the following areas:

- Business Partners
- Cultural Information
- Funding Agencies
- Information Resources
- National Language Organizations
- National Language Resource Centers
- Regional Language Associations
- Search Engines
- State Departments of Education
- State Language Associations
- State Language Frameworks
- Year of Languages

National Association of District Supervisors of Foreign Languages (NADSFL)

www.nadsfl.org

NADSFL gives support to department heads and district-level coordinators of world language programs.

National Council of State Supervisors for Languages (NCSSFL)

www.ncssfl.org

NCSSFL provides annual state-by-state reports on world language legislation, policies, and initiatives; position papers on critical issues affecting language learning; links to state world language standards and frameworks; and contact information for state supervisors.

Alliance for the Advancement of Heritage Languages

www.cal.org/heritage

This alliance promotes the conservation and development of the heritage-language resources of the United States in order to produce citizens who can function professionally in English and other languages.

Language-Specific Organizations

The following national language-specific organizations provide support to language teachers through professional development, advocacy, and resources for teaching. These organizations represent the languages more commonly taught in schools in the United States.

American Association of Teachers of Arabic

www.wm.edu/aata

American Association of Teachers of French

www.frenchteachers.org

American Association of Teachers of German

www.aatg.org

American Association of Teachers of Italian

www.aati-online.org

American Association of Teachers of Slavic and East European Languages
www.aatseel.org

American Association of Teachers of Spanish and Portuguese
www.aatsp.org

American Classical League (for teachers of Latin and Greek)
www.aclclassics.org

American Council of Teachers of Russian
www.americancouncils.org

Chinese Language Teachers Association
www.clta.osu.edu

National Council of Japanese Language Teachers (NCJLT)
www.ncjlt.org

Regional Language Organizations

These five organizations provide professional development at a regional level and work with and through state organizations of language educators.

Central States Conference on the Teaching of Foreign Languages
www.centralstates.cc

Northeast Conference on the Teaching of Foreign Languages
http://omega.dickinson.edu/nectfl

Pacific Northwest Council for Languages
http://babel.uoregon.edu/pncfl

Southern Conference on Language Teaching
www.valdosta.edu/scolt

Southwest Conference on Language Teaching
www.swcolt.org

National Language Resource Centers

Foreign Language Resource Centers
http://nflrc.msu.edu

The U.S. Department of Education has awarded grants to a small number of institutions for the purpose of establishing, strengthening, and operating national foreign language resource and training centers to improve the teaching and learning of foreign languages. Currently, 15 Title VI Language Resource Centers exist nationwide, each with a particular area of concentration.

Center for Advanced Language Proficiency Education and Research (CALPER), Pennsylvania State University
www.calper.la.psu.edu

CALPER focuses on improving the environment of advanced-level foreign language teaching, learning, and assessment. It conducts research, develops teaching and learning materials, and provides educational opportunities for language professionals.

Center for Advanced Research on Language Acquisition (CARLA), University of Minnesota
www.carla.umn.edu

CARLA studies multilingualism and multiculturalism to develop knowledge of second-language acquisition and to advance the quality of second-language teaching, learning, and assessment. CARLA offers a number of resources to language teachers, including a battery of second-language proficiency assessments and a series of working papers.

Center for Applied Second Language Studies (CASLS), University of Oregon
http://casls.uoregon.edu/home.php

CASLS promotes international literacy by supporting communities of educators and by partnering with those communities to develop a comprehensive system of proficiency-based tools for lifelong language learning and teaching. CASLS works with K–16 teams of teachers to develop content-based thematic units, including authentic materials and performance assessments.

Center for Educational Resources in Culture, Language and Literacy (CERCLL), University of Arizona

www.cercll.arizona.edu

CERCLL serves as a unique local, regional, and national resource for scholars, academic professionals, teachers-and others interested in improving our nation's capacity to deliver high-quality, pedagogically sound, and cost-effective instruction in foreign languages.

Center for Language Education and Research (CLEAR), Michigan State University

www.clear.msu.edu

CLEAR develops materials and conducts research for foreign language teaching and learning and provides professional development opportunities for educators in the field. Projects relate to classroom practice and address commonalities across languages.

Center for Languages of the Central Asian Region (CELCAR), Indiana University

www.indiana.edu/~celcar

CELCAR seeks to enhance U.S. national capacity for teaching and learning the languages and cultures of Central Asia and surrounding regions.

Language Acquisition Resource Center (LARC), San Diego State University

http://larcnet.sdsu.edu

LARC develops and supports the teaching and learning of foreign languages in the United States through research, technology, and publications. Particular attention is paid to less commonly taught languages, cross-cultural issues, language skills assessment, and teacher training.

National African Language Resource Center (NALRC), University of Wisconsin

http://african.lss.wisc.edu/nalrc

NALRC serves the entire community of African language educators and learners in the United States by sponsoring a wide range of educational and professional activities designed to improve the accessibility and quality of African language instruction in the United States.

National Capital Language Resource Center (NCLRC), Georgetown University Center for Applied Linguistics

www.nclrc.org

NCLRC serves as a resource to improve the teaching and learning of foreign languages by providing material resources and professional services that derive from its activities and projects. It publishes a monthly electronic newsletter and online resources for the teaching of culture in a variety of languages.

National East Asian Languages Resource Center (NEALRC), Ohio State University

www.flc.osu.edu

NEALRC serves the needs of learners and teachers of East Asian languages through initiatives designed to increase learners' abilities to master advanced levels of language and cultural competence.

National Foreign Language Resource Center (NFLRC), University of Hawaii at Manoa

www.nflrc.hawaii.edu

NFLRC undertakes projects that focus primarily on the less commonly taught languages of East Asia, Southeast Asia, and the Pacific. Many of its projects have implications for the teaching and learning of all languages and have the overriding goal of developing prototypes that can be applied broadly as resources to improve foreign language education nationally.

National K–12 Foreign Language Resource Center (NFLRC), Iowa State University

www.hs.iastate.edu

NFLRC's mission is to improve student learning of foreign languages in kindergarten through 12th grade throughout the United States. NFLRC is well known nationally for its excellent summer institutes, publications, and research.

National Middle East Language Resource Center (NMELRC), Brigham Young University

http://nmelrc.byu.edu

NMELRC coordinates efforts aimed at increasing and improving opportunities for learning the languages of the Middle East. The center undertakes and supports teacher training, materials development, testing and assessment, integration of pedagogy and technology, study abroad, and K–12 programs.

Slavic and East European Language Resource Center (SEELRC), Duke University & University of North Carolina

www.seelrc.org

SEELRC's goal is to improve the national capacity to teach and learn Slavic and East European languages by developing teaching and assessment materials and by supporting research and other activities, including undergraduate and graduate education and exchange programs, conferences, seminars, and public outreach programs.

South Asia Language Resource Center (SALRC), University of Chicago

http://salrc.uchicago.edu

SALRC is the umbrella organization under which less commonly taught languages are advanced through a coordinated program to improve the national infrastructure for language teaching and learning. It creates and disseminates new resources for teaching and research with other institutions having overlapping language interests, most notably those for the Middle East and Central Asia.

Policy and Advocacy

International Ed.org

www.internationaled.org

International Ed.org is a Web site that provides curricular resources, research, and information on initiatives that support international studies in schools. It provides resources that support efforts to increase knowledge about other world regions and cultures, other languages, and international issues. The site contains links to international projects and activities in the United States and information on new programs related to critical-need languages.

Joint National Committee for Languages and the National Council for Languages and International Studies (JNCL-NCLIS)

www.languagepolicy.org

JNCL is a coalition of more than 60 organizations that encompasses virtually all areas of the language profession. It functions as a point of reference for the identification of national needs and the planning of national language policies. NCLIS is a registered lobbying organization and serves as the "action arm" for the language and international education communities. The Web site contains valuable links and information on advocacy and federal and state legislation affecting language programs.

Minnesota New Visions: Languages for Life

www.mctlc.org/newvisions/prresources.html

This Web site includes links and information about a variety of resources, including brochures and videos that promote language learning, articles and reports that give background information and overviews on language learning, databases of information on language learning, advocacy resources; and other resources for language teachers.

2004 National Language Conference

www.nlconference.org

This site contains papers presented at the National Language Conference in 2004 by experts in government, business, and education that offer examples of international best practices, models for K–16 language education, and state and national language policies. As of March 2007, no additional national language conferences have been held.)

New Visions in Action: Foreign Language Education
www.hs.iastate.edu/

New Visions in Action has coordinated the work of numerous world language organizations to create common purpose and effective efforts focusing on curriculum, instruction, articulation and assessment, second-language research, and teacher recruitment and retention. The project's Web site offers checklists with criteria of excellence to guide program planners and implementers.

Office of English Language Acquisition, Language Enhancement, and Academic Achievement for Limited English Proficient Students
www.ed.gov/about/offices/list/oela

OELA's primary goal is to identify major issues affecting the education of English language learners. OELA also is the program office for foreign language instruction and administers the Foreign Language Assistance Program (FLAP). This program makes available grants to pay for the federal share of the cost of innovative model programs providing for the establishment, improvement, or expansion of foreign language study for elementary and secondary school students.

The Alliance for Language Learning
www.allianceforlanguagelearning.org

The Alliance for Language Learning is an advocacy group made up of business, higher education, and community leaders in North Carolina that sponsors North Carolina's K–12 articulation program, VISION 2010. The Web site contains examples of models of articulation and other resources.

The European Centre for Modern Languages
www.ecml.at

This site contains information on the implementation of language policies and the promotion of innovative approaches to the learning and teaching of modern languages.

Year of Languages
www.yearoflanguages.org

Year of Languages is a national advocacy effort designed to create public interest in and support for learning languages. Activities during the year 2005 celebrated and highlighted language diversity and opportunities to learn languages from elementary grades through adulthood. These activities began a decade-long emphasis, through 2015, on the goal of realizing the vision of languages for all.

Early Language Learning

Language Study and the Brain
www.teresakennedy.com/

This site provides information on the relationship of brain research to effective foreign language instruction at the elementary level and after puberty.

Ñandu
www.cal.org/earlylang/

Ñandu is a listserv for school district personnel, superintendents, teachers, college and university teacher educators, and parents. It is sponsored by the Improving Foreign Language Instruction Project of the Northeast and Islands Regional Educational Laboratory at Brown University (LAB) and is funded by the U.S. Department of Education.

Ñandutí
www.cal.org/earlylang

Available through the same site as Ñandu, Ñandutí is a resource on foreign language learning in grades K–8 that offers information on the benefits of early foreign language learning, advocacy, how to start a K–8 program, integrating content into language instruction, using technology, and assessing student progress. It also contains a national directory of early language learning programs.

National Network for Early Language Learning (NNELL)

www.nnell.org

NNELL is an organization for educators involved in teaching world languages to children. NNELL provides leadership, support, and service to those committed to early language learning and coordinates efforts to make language learning in programs of excellence a reality for all children. NNELL publishes the journal *Learning Languages* twice a year. The Members Only section of the Web site contains a detailed Members Directory, a subsection on advocacy, a message board, access to classroom activities and lesson plans, and a complete subsection on building an early language-learning program.

Support for Elementary Educators Through Distance Education in Spanish (SEEDS)

http://seeds.coedu.usf.edu/index2.htm

This Title VI federal grant project is designed to develop three distance-education modules, available on CD-ROM and through the Web. The modules are (1) Spanish Enhancement, (2) Teaching Spanish as a Foreign Language, and (3) Internationalizing the Elementary Curriculum.

The Balanced Curriculum: A Guiding Document for Scheduling and Implementation of the NC Standard Course of Study at the Elementary Level

www.ncpublicschools.org/curriculum

This document (available in PDF format only—requires Adobe Acrobat) from the North Carolina Department of Public Instruction focuses on the importance and value of a well-rounded education that includes learning languages. The document provides guiding principles and recommendations, sample scenarios and schedules, and resources to implement such a curriculum.

The GLOBE Program
www.globe.gov

The GLOBE Program is a worldwide, hands-on, primary and secondary school-based education and science program that can be used to integrate science concepts into the world language classroom. The Web site links to a number of sites with information, activities, and opportunities related to the goals of the GLOBE Program.

Language Teaching Resources

Bibliography of Modern Foreign Languages and Special Education Needs
www.specialeducationalneeds.com

This 2004 international bibliography contains valuable resources on special-needs students in second-language programs at all levels of instruction. Topics include students with cognitive and learning needs, emotional and behavioral needs, and sensory and physical needs. (Note: The URL provided leads to the professional page of the bibliography's author, David R. Wilson. Scroll down the page to select the link titled "Bibliographies of special educational needs in school subject teaching," located under "Word Documents." Accessing this page leads to a list of subject area links, including "Modern Foreign Languages," which opens a Microsoft Word file.)

Center for Applied Linguistics
www.cal.org

The center creates publications, conducts research, gathers articles and information, and develops projects to further the teaching and learning of languages in a variety of settings: language courses for English speakers; K–12 immersion programs, including dual-language immersion and content-based immersion; bilingual education; and teaching English as a second language.

Content-Based Language Teaching with Technology (CoBaLTT)

www.carla.umn.edu/cobaltt

This Web site features lesson plans and units developed by teachers during yearlong professional development projects on standards- and content-based instruction and curriculum.

Computer Assisted Language Instruction Consortium (CALICO)

www.calico.org

This professional organization focuses on both education and technology, with an emphasis on language teaching and learning. The Web site features a clearinghouse of information on computer-assisted language learning.

Education Resources Information Center (ERIC)

www.eric.ed.gov

ERIC is a digital library consisting primarily of electronic bibliographic records describing journal and nonjournal literature on education topics, including languages and linguistics, from 1966 to the present. The site provides extensive search functionality by topic as well as an electronic question-and-answer service, Ask ERIC.

Foreign Language Teaching Forum (FL Teach)

www.cortland.edu/flteach

This listserv connects more than 4,000 educators, mainly in the United States but also in 60 other countries, to discuss issues in teaching languages at all levels, including school/college articulation, training of student teachers, classroom activities, curriculum, and syllabus design. Participants—including preservice teacher candidates, methods professors, new and veteran teachers, and administrators—also have access to an extensive archive.

Foreign Embassies of Washington, D.C.

www.embassy.org/embassies

The staff of Foreign Embassies of Washington, D.C., often develop classroom resources and offer study opportunities for language teachers through their education offices. This site maintains updated listings of Web sites for embassies of foreign governments in the United States.

Fulbright Teacher and Administrator Exchange Program

www.fulbrightexchanges.org

This organization coordinates programs to bring educators from other countries for short- and long-term study seminars in the United States and for U.S. educators to learn abroad through focused study projects.

International Association for Language Learning Technology

www.iallt.org/

This association provides leadership in the development, integration, evaluation, and management of instructional technology for the teaching and learning of languages, literature, and culture.

International Education and Resource Network (iEARN)

www.iearn.org

This online, project-based network of schools links students and teachers from more than 100 countries around the world.

The Virtual Assessment Center

www.carla.umn.edu/assessment/vac

This professional development module guides teachers through the creation of performance assessments for use in their classrooms.

Appendix
ACTFL Performance Guidelines
for K–12 Learners

Novice Learner Range (Grades K–4, 5–8, or 9–10)

Comprehensibility: How well are they understood?

Interpersonal
- Rely primarily on memorized phrases and short sentences during highly predictable interactions on very familiar topics.
- Are understood primarily by those very accustomed to interacting with language learners.
- Imitate modeled words and phrases using intonation and pronunciation similar to that of the model.
- May show evidence of false starts, prolonged and unexpectedly placed pauses, and recourse to their native language as topics expand beyond the scope of immediate needs.
- Are able to meet limited practical writing needs, such as short messages and notes, by recombining learned vocabulary and structure to form simple sentences on very familiar topics.

Presentational
- Use short, memorized phrases and sentences in oral and written presentations.
- Are understood primarily by those who are very accustomed to interacting with language learners.
- Demonstrate some accuracy in pronunciation and intonation when presenting well-rehearsed material on familiar topics.

• May show evidence of false starts, prolonged and unexpectedly placed pauses, and recourse to their native language as topics expand beyond the scope of immediate needs.
    • Show abilities in writing by reproducing familiar material.
    • Rely heavily on visuals to enhance comprehensibility in both oral and written presentations.

Comprehension: How well do they understand?

Interpersonal
    • Comprehend general information and vocabulary when the communication partner uses objects, visuals, and gestures in speaking or writing.
    • Generally need contextual clues, redundancy, paraphrasing, or restatement in order to understand the message.

Interpretive
    • Understand short, simple conversations and narratives (live and recorded material) within highly predictable and familiar contexts.
    • Rely on personal background experience to assist in comprehension.
    • Exhibit increased comprehension when constructing meaning through recognition of key words or phrases embedded in familiar contexts.
    • Comprehend written and spoken language better when content has been previously presented in an oral and/or visual context.
    • Determine meaning by recognition of cognates, prefixes, and thematic vocabulary.

Language Control: How accurate is their language?

Interpersonal
    • Comprehend messages that include predominately familiar grammatical structures.

• Are most accurate when communicating about very familiar topics using memorized oral and written phrases.

• Exhibit decreased accuracy when attempting to create with the language.

• Write with accuracy when copying written language but may use invented spelling when writing words or producing characters on their own.

• May exhibit frequent errors in capitalization and punctuation when target language differs from native language in these areas.

Interpretive

• Recognize structural patterns in target language narratives and derive meaning from these structures within familiar contexts.

• Sometimes recognize previously learned structures when presented in new contexts.

Presentational

• Demonstrate some accuracy in oral and written presentations when reproducing memorized words, phrases, and sentences in the target language.

• Formulate oral and written presentations using a limited range of simple phrases and expressions based on very familiar topics.

• Show inaccuracies or interference from the native language when attempting to communicate information that goes beyond the memorized or prefabricated.

• May exhibit frequent errors in capitalization, punctuation, or production of characters when the writing system of the target language differs from the native language.

Vocabulary Use: How extensive and applicable is their vocabulary?

Interpersonal

• Comprehend and produce vocabulary that is related to everyday objects and actions on a limited number of familiar topics.

• Use words and phrases primarily as lexical items without awareness of grammatical structure.

• Recognize and use vocabulary from a variety of topics, including those related to other curricular areas.

• May often rely on words and phrases from their native language when attempting to communicate beyond the word or gesture level.

Interpretive

• Recognize a variety of vocabulary words and expressions related to familiar topics embedded within relevant curricular areas.

• Demonstrate increased comprehension of vocabulary in spoken passages when enhanced by pantomime, props, or visuals.

• Demonstrate increased comprehension of written passages when accompanied by illustrations and other contextual clues.

Presentational

• Use a limited number of words and phrases for common objects and actions in familiar categories.

• Supplement their basic vocabulary with expressions acquired from sources such as the teacher or picture dictionaries.

• Rely on native language words and phrases when expressing personal meaning in less familiar categories.

Communication Strategies: How do they maintain communication?

Interpersonal

• Attempt to clarify meaning by repeating words and occasionally selecting substitute words to convey their message.

• Primarily use facial expressions and gestures to indicate problems with comprehension.

Interpretive

• Use background experience to anticipate story direction in highly predictable oral or written texts.

• Rely heavily on visuals and familiar language to assist in comprehension.

Presentational

• Make corrections by repeating or rewriting when appropriate forms are routinely modeled by the teacher.

• Rely heavily on repetition, nonverbal expression (gestures, facial expressions), and visuals to communicate their message.

Cultural Awareness: How is their cultural understanding reflected in their communication?

Interpersonal

• Imitate culturally appropriate vocabulary and idiomatic expressions.

• Use gestures and body language that are generally those of their own culture, unless they are incorporated into memorized responses.

Interpretive

• Understand both oral and written language that reflects a cultural background similar to their own.

• Predict a story line or event when it reflects a cultural background similar to their own.

Presentational

• Imitate the use of culturally appropriate vocabulary, idiomatic expressions, and nonverbal behaviors modeled by the teacher.

Intermediate Learner Range (Grades K–8, 5–12, or 9–12)

Comprehensibility: How well are they understood?

Interpersonal

• Express their own thoughts using sentences and strings of sentences when interacting on familiar topics in present time.

- Are understood by those accustomed to interacting with language learners.
- Use pronunciation and intonation patterns that can be understood by a native speaker accustomed to interacting with language learners.
- Make false starts and pause frequently to search for words when interacting with others.
- Are able to meet practical writing needs, such as short letters and notes, by recombining learned vocabulary and structures. Demonstrate full control of present time and evidence of some control of other time frames.

Presentational

- Express, describe, and narrate their own thoughts using sentences and strings of sentences in oral and written presentations on familiar topics.
- Use pronunciation and intonation patterns that can be understood by those accustomed to interacting with language learners.
- Make false starts and pause frequently to search for words when interacting with others.
- Communicate oral and written information about familiar topics with sufficient accuracy so that listeners and readers understand most of what is presented.

Comprehension: How well do they understand?

Interpersonal

- Comprehend general concepts and messages about familiar and occasionally unfamiliar topics.
- May not comprehend details when dealing with unfamiliar topics.
- May have difficulty comprehending language supported by situational context.

Interpretive

- Understand longer, more complex conversations and narratives as well as recorded material in familiar contexts.

• Use background knowledge to comprehend simple stories, personal correspondence, and other contextualized print.

• Identify main ideas and some specific information on a limited number of topics found in the products of the target culture, such as those presented on TV, radio, and live and computer-generated presentations, although comprehension may be uneven.

• Determine meaning by using contextual clues.

• Are aided by the use of redundancy, paraphrasing, and restatement in order to understand the message.

Language Control: How accurate is their language?

Interpersonal

• Comprehend messages that include some unfamiliar grammatical structures.

• Are most accurate when creating with the language about familiar topics in present time using simple sentences or strings of sentences.

• Exhibit a decline in grammatical accuracy as creativity in language production increases.

• Begin to apply familiar structures to new situations.

• Show evidence of awareness of capitalization and punctuation when writing in the target language.

• Recognize some of their own spelling or character production errors and make appropriate adjustments.

Interpretive

• Derive meaning by comparing target language structures with those of the native language.

• Recognize parallels between new and familiar structures in the target language.

• Understand high-frequency idiomatic expressions.

Presentational

• Formulate oral and written presentations on familiar topics using a range of sentences and strings of sentences, primarily in present time but also, with preparation, in past and future time.

• May show inaccuracies as well as some interference from the native language when attempting to present less familiar material.

• Exhibit fairly good accuracy in capitalization and punctuation (or production of characters) when target language differs from native language in these areas.

Vocabulary Use: How extensive and applicable is their vocabulary?

Interpersonal

• Use vocabulary from a variety of thematic groups.

• Recognize and use vocabulary from a variety of topics, including those related to other curricular areas.

• Show some understanding and use of common idiomatic expressions.

• May use false cognates or resort to their native language when attempting to communicate beyond the scope of familiar topics.

Interpretive

• Comprehend an expanded range of vocabulary.

• Frequently derive meaning of unknown words by using contextual clues.

• Demonstrate enhanced comprehension when listening to or reading content that has a recognizable format.

Presentational

• Demonstrate control of an expanding number of familiar words and phrases and of a limited number of idiomatic expressions.

• Supplement their basic vocabulary for both oral and written presentations with expressions acquired from other sources such as dictionaries.

• In speech and writing may sometimes use false cognates and incorrectly applied terms and show only partial control of newly acquired expressions.

Communication Strategies: How do they maintain communication?

Interpersonal
   • May use paraphrasing, question asking, circumlocution, and other strategies to avoid a breakdown in communication.
   • Attempt to self-correct, primarily for meaning, when communication breaks down.

Interpretive
   • Identify the main idea of a written text by using reading strategies such as gleaning information from the first and last paragraphs.
   • Infer meaning of many unfamiliar words that are necessary in order to understand the gist of an oral or written text.
   • Use contextual clues to assist in comprehension.

Presentational
   • Make occasional use of reference sources and efforts at self-correction to avoid errors likely to interfere with communication.
   • Use circumlocution when faced with difficult syntactic structures, problematic spelling, or unfamiliar vocabulary.
   • Make use of memory aids (such as notes and visuals) to facilitate presentations.

Cultural Awareness: How is their cultural understanding reflected in their communication?

Interpersonal
   • Use some culturally appropriate vocabulary and idiomatic expressions.
   • Use some gestures and body language of the target culture.

Interpretive
   • Use knowledge of their own culture and that of the target culture(s) to interpret oral or written texts more accurately.
   • Recognize target culture influences in the products and practices of their own culture.

• Recognize differences and similarities in the perspectives of the target culture and their own.

Presentational

• Use some culturally appropriate vocabulary, idiomatic expressions, and nonverbal behaviors.

• Demonstrate some cultural knowledge in oral and written presentations.

Preadvanced Learner Range (Grades K–12)

Comprehensibility: How well are they understood?

Interpersonal

• Narrate and describe using connected sentences and paragraphs in present and other time frames when interacting with topics of personal, school, and community interest.

• Are understood by those with whom they interact, although a range of linguistic inaccuracies may still exist, and, on occasion, the communication partner may need to make a special effort to understand the message.

• Use pronunciation and intonation patterns that are understandable to a native speaker unaccustomed to interacting with language learners.

• Use language confidently and with ease, with few pauses.

• Are able to meet practical writing needs such as letters and summaries by writing descriptions and narrations of paragraph length and organization, showing sustained control of basic structures and partial control of more complex structures and time frames.

Presentational

• Report, narrate, and describe using connected sentences and paragraph-length or longer discourse in oral and written presentations on topics of personal, school, and community interest.

• Use pronunciation and intonation patterns that are understood by native users of the language, although the listener/reader may on occasion need to make a special effort to understand the message.

• Use language confidently and with ease, with few pauses.

• Communicate with a fairly high degree of facility when making oral and written presentations about familiar and well-researched topics.

Comprehension: How well do they understand?

Interpersonal

• Comprehend main ideas and most details on a variety of topics beyond the immediate situation.

• Occasionally do not comprehend but usually are able to clarify details by asking questions.

• May encounter difficulty comprehending language dealing with abstract topics.

Interpretive

• Use knowledge acquired in other settings and from other curricular areas to comprehend both spoken and written messages.

• Understand main ideas and significant details on a variety of topics found in the products of the target culture, such as those presented on TV, radio, video, or in live and computer-generated presentations, although comprehension may be uneven.

• Develop an awareness of tone, style, and author perspective.

• Demonstrate a growing independence as a reader or listener and generally comprehend what they read and hear without relying solely on formally learned vocabulary.

Language Control: How accurate is their language?

Interpersonal

• Comprehend messages that include unfamiliar grammatical structures.

- Are most accurate when narrating and describing in connected sentences and paragraphs in present time, with decreasing accuracy in past and future times.
- May continue to exhibit inaccuracies as the amount and complexity of language increases.
- Communicate successfully by applying familiar structures to new situations.
- Rarely make errors in capitalization and in punctuation.
- Are generally accurate in spelling or production of characters.

Interpretive

- Deduce meaning in unfamiliar language passages by classifying words or concepts according to word order or grammatical use.
- Apply rules of language to construct meaning from oral and written texts.
- Understand idiomatic expressions.
- Move beyond literal comprehension toward more critical reading and listening.

Presentational

- Accurately formulate paragraph-length and longer oral and written presentations in present time on topics of personal, school, community, and global interest.
- May show some inaccuracies or interferences from the native language when presentations deal with multiple time frames or other complex structures.
- Successfully communicate personal meaning by applying familiar structures to new situations and less familiar topics, and by integrating information from audio, visual, and written sources.
- Exhibit awareness of the need for accuracy in capitalization and punctuation (or production of characters) when target language differs from native language in these areas.

Vocabulary Use: How extensive and applicable is their vocabulary?

Interpersonal

• Understand and often use idiomatic and culturally authentic expressions.

• Recognize and use vocabulary from a variety of topics, including those related to other curricular areas.

• Use more specialized and precise vocabulary terms within a limited number of topics.

Interpretive

• Comprehend a wide range of vocabulary in both concrete and abstract contexts. Infer meaning of both oral and written texts by recognizing familiar words and phrases in new contexts.

• Use context to deduce meaning of unfamiliar vocabulary.

• Recognize and understand the cultural context of many words and phrases.

Presentational

• Demonstrate control of an extensive vocabulary, including a number of idiomatic and culturally authentic expressions from a variety of topics.

• Supplement their basic vocabulary by using resources such as textbooks and dictionaries.

• May use more specialized and precise terms when dealing with specific topics that have been researched.

Communication Strategies: How do they maintain communication?

Interpersonal

• Are able to sustain an interaction with a native speaker by using a variety of strategies when discussion topics relate to personal experience or immediate needs.

• Show evidence of attention to mechanical errors even when these may not interfere with communication.

Interpretive
• Use background knowledge to deduce meaning and to understand complex information in oral or written texts.
• Identify the organizing principle(s) of oral or written texts.
• Infer and interpret the intent of the writer.

Presentational
• Demonstrate conscious efforts at correct formulation and self-correction by use of self-editing and reference sources.
• Sustain length and continuity of presentations by appropriate use of strategies such as simplification, reformulation, and circumlocution.
• Make use of a variety of resource materials and presentation methods to enhance presentations.

Cultural Awareness: How is their cultural understanding reflected in their communication?

Interpersonal
• Use culturally appropriate vocabulary and idioms.
• Use appropriate gestures and body language of the target culture.

Interpretive
• Apply understanding of the target culture to enhance comprehension of oral and written texts.
• Recognize the reflections of practices, products, and perspectives of the target cultures(s) in oral and written texts.
• Analyze and evaluate cultural stereotypes encountered in oral and written texts.

Presentational
• Demonstrate increased use of culturally appropriate vocabulary, idiomatic expressions, and nonverbal behaviors.
• Use language increasingly reflective of authentic cultural practices and perspectives.

References

American Council on Education. (2002). *Beyond September 11: A comprehensive national policy on international education*. Washington, DC: Author.

American Council on the Teaching of Foreign Languages. (1996). *Standards for foreign language learning: Preparing for the 21st Century*. Yonkers, NY: Author.

American Council on the Teaching of Foreign Languages. (1999). *ACTFL performance guidelines for K–12 learners*. Yonkers, NY: Author.

Annenberg/Corporation for Public Broadcasting. (2003a). *Teaching foreign languages K–12: A library of classroom practices*. [Pamphlet]. Boston: WGBH Educational Foundation in conjunction with the American Council on the Teaching of Foreign Languages.

Annenberg/Corporation for Public Broadcasting. (2003b). *Teaching foreign languages K–12: A library of classroom practices*. Retrieved April 26, 2005, from www.learner.org/channel/libraries/tfl

Bales, S. N. (2004, January). *Making the public case for international education: A FrameWorks message memo* (pp. 1–19). Washington, DC: FrameWorks Institute.

Castaing, M. (2002, November). *States institute on international education in the schools: Institute report*. New York: The Asia Society.

Center for Advanced Research on Language Acquisition. (2003). *Minnesota language proficiency assessments*. Minneapolis: University of Minnesota.

Clementi, D. (2004, September 27). *World languages: Communicating important ideas*. Workshop presented for the New Jersey Department of Education in Monroe Township, N.J.

Council of Chief State School Officers. (2004). *Surveys of enacted curriculum*. Retrieved April 26, 2005, from www.ccsso.org /projects/Surveys_of_ Enacted_Curriculum

Council of Europe. (2001). *A common European framework of reference for languages*. Retrieved April 26, 2005, from www.culture2.coe.int/portfolio/ documents_intro /common_framework.html

Curtain, H., & Dahlberg, C. A. (2004). *Key concepts for success: Elementary and middle school foreign languages* (pp. xiv-xv). Boston: Pearson Education, Inc.

De Mado, J. (1995). *Inclusion in the language classroom* [audiocassette]. Washington, CT: John De Mado Language Seminars, Inc.

Diaz-Maggioli, G. (2004). *A passion for learning: Teacher-centered professional development.* Alexandria, VA: Association for Supervision and Curriculum Development.

Doggett, G. (2003). *Eight approaches to language teaching.* CAL Digest Series 1: Complete Collection, p. 168. Washington, DC: Center for Applied Linguistics.

Donato, R. (1998). Assessing foreign language abilities of the early language learner. In M. Met (Ed.), *Critical issues in early second language learning* (pp. 169–175). Glenview, IL: Scott Foresman-Addison Wesley.

Donato, R. (2000). Building knowledge, building leaders: Collaborating for research and change. In L. M. Wallinger (Ed.), *Teaching in changing times: The courage to lead.* (Northeast Conference Reports, pp. 89–119). New York: McGraw-Hill Higher Education.

Duff, P. (2004, January 12-14). *Foreign language policies, research, and educational possibilities: A western perspective.* Paper presented at the APEC Educational Summit in Beijing.

Friedman, T. (1999) *The Lexus and the olive tree.* New York: Farrar, Straus, Giroux.

Fullan, M. (2002). The change leader. *Educational Leadership, 59*(8), 16–20.

Gardner, H. (1983). *Frames of mind: The theory of multiple intelligences.* New York: Basic.

Gifford, C. (2004, April 14). *Spanish for the professions: Getting the job done.* Presentation given at the Northeast Conference on the Teaching of Foreign Languages.

Gilzow, D. F., & Branaman, L. E. (2000). *Lessons learned: Model foreign language programs.* Washington, DC: The Center for Applied Linguistics and Delta Systems.

Hayward, F. M., & Siaya, L. M. (2001). *A report on two national surveys about international education.* Washington, DC: American Council on Education.

Jensen, J. (2002). Supervisors as agents of change: Creating innovative structures to support teaching and learning. *New Jersey Journal of Supervision and Curriculum Development, 46,* 43–68.

Jensen, J. (2004). [Informal electronic survey of the National Council of State Supervisors for Languages]. Unpublished raw data.

Keatley, C. (2004, March). Who is paying the bills? The federal budget and foreign language education in U.S. schools and universities. *The national language resource newsletter*. Retrieved March 7, 2005, from www.nclrc.org/caidlr82.htm

Kennedy, T. J. (1999, Spring). GLOBE integrates mathematics, science, social studies, and technology into the foreign language classroom. *Learning Languages, 4*(3), 23–25.

Kennedy, T. J., & Canney, G. (2000). Collaborating across language, age, and geographic borders. In K. Risko & K. Bromley (Eds.), *Collaboration for diverse learners: Viewpoints and practices* (pp. 310–329). Newark, DE: International Reading Association.

Kenyon, D., Farr, B., Mitchell, J., & Armengol, R. (2000). *Framework for the 2004 foreign language national assessment of educational progress*. Washington, DC: National Assessment Governing Board.

Language Learning Solutions. (2003). *Standards-based measurement of proficiency*. Retrieved April 26, 2005, from www.onlinells.com/onlinells/stamp.asp

Little, D., & Perclova, R. (2002). *The European language portfolio: A guide for teachers and teacher trainers*. Strasbourg, France: Council of Europe.

Moeller, A., Scow, V., & Van Houten, J. B. (2005). Documenting and improving student learning through linguafolios. In P. Boyles & P. Sandrock (Eds.), *The year of languages: challenges, changes, and choices*. Milwaukee, WI: Central States Conference on the Teaching of Foreign Languages.

Mok, S. (2004). Address by the Honorable Sam Mok, chief financial officer, U.S. Department of Labor, to the National Language Conference on June 23, 2004, at the University of Maryland.

National Association of District Supervisors of Foreign Languages. (1999). *Characteristics of effective foreign language instruction*. Retrieved April 26, 2005, from www.nadsfl.org/characteristics.htm

National Association of District Supervisors of Foreign Languages. (n.d.). *The language supervisor: An indispensable part of a quality language program*. Retrieved April 26, 2005, from www.nadsfl.org/qualityprogram

National Association of State Boards of Education. (2003, October). *The complete curriculum: Ensuring a place for the arts and foreign languages in America's schools*. Alexandria, VA: Author.

National Board for Professional Teaching Standards. (2001). *World languages other than english standards*. Washington, DC: Author.

National Commission on Asia in the Schools. (2001, June). *Asia in the schools: Preparing young Americans for today's interconnected world*. New York: The Asia Society.

National Council of State Supervisors for Languages (2002). *Foreign language education for all students: A position paper.* Retrieved March 3, 2005, from www.ncssfl.org/papers/index.php?allstudents.

National Standards in Foreign Language Education Project. (1996). *Standards for foreign language learning: Preparing for the 21st century.* Yonkers, NY: Author.

National Standards in Foreign Language Education Project. (1999). *Standards for foreign language learning in the 21st century.* Lawrence, KS: Allen Press, Inc.

National Virtual Translation Center. (2004). *Languages of the world.* Retrieved April 26, 2005, from www.nvtc.gov/lotw/months/november/USschoollanguages.htm

Nebraska Department of Education. (1996). *Nebraska K–12 foreign language frameworks.* Lincoln, NE: Author.

New Jersey Department of Education. (1999). *New Jersey world languages curriculum framework.* Trenton, NJ: Author.

New Jersey Department of Education. (2004). *Academic and professional standards: World languages.* Retrieved April 26, 2005, from www.state.nj.us/njded/aps/cccs/wl/regs.htm

Power, C. (2005). Not the Queen's English: Non-native English speakers now outnumber native ones 3 to 1 and it's changing the way we communicate. *Newsweek International,* 46.

Samaniego, F., & Pino, C. (2000). Frequently asked questions about SNS programs. In N. Anderson (Ed.), *AATSP professional development series handbook for teachers K–16, volume I: Spanish for native speakers* (pp. 29–64). Fort Worth, TX: Harcourt College.

Sandrock, P., & Wang, S. (2005, March). Building an infrastructure to meet the language needs of all children. *The State Standard.* Alexandria, VA: National Association of State Boards of Education.

Shuler, S. C. (2003, Fall). When no curriculum is left balanced, the needs of the children are left behind. *Connecticut Journal of Educational Leadership, 1,* 45–52.

Sparks, D. (2002). *Designing powerful staff development for teachers and principals.* Oxford, OH: National Staff Development Council.

Sparks, D. (2004, August 11). *Leading for results: Transforming teaching, learning and relationships in schools.* Presentation given to the New Jersey Professional Teachers Standards Board.

Spinelli, E., & Nerenz, A. G. (2004, Spring). Learning scenarios: The new foreign language curriculum. *CLEAR News, 8*(1), 1–6.

U.S. Department of Defense. (2004). *A call to action for national foreign language capabilities.* Draft white paper. Washington, DC: Author.

Valdes, G. (2001). Heritage language students: Profiles and possibilities. In J. K. Peyton, D. Ranard, & S. McGinnis (Eds.), *Heritage languages in America: Preserving a national resource* (pp. 37–77). McHenry, IL: Delta Systems; and Washington, DC: Center for Applied Linguistics.

von Zastrow, C. (2004, March). *Academic atrophy: The condition of the liberal arts in America's public schools.* Washington, DC: Council for Basic Education.

Wilcox, J. (2006). Foreign language learning gap concerns U.S. leaders. *Education Update, 48*(5). Alexandria, VA: Association for Supervision and Curriculum Development.

Zimmer-Loew, H. (2000). Professional development and change. In R. M. Terry & F. W. Medley (Eds.), *Agents of change in a changing age* (pp. 169–209). Lincoln Wood, IL: National Textbook Company.

Index

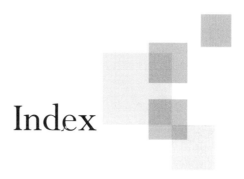

Note: Entries followed by an *f* denote figures.

Related ASCD Resources

At the time of publication, the following ASCD resources were available (ASCD stock numbers appear in parentheses). For up-to-date information about ASCD resources, go to www.ascd.org.

Networks

Visit the ASCD Web site (www.ascd.org) and click on About ASCD. Click on Networks for information about professional educators who have formed groups around topics like "Language, Literacy, and Literature." Look in the "Network Directory" for current facilitators' addresses and phone numbers.

Print Products

Other books in the Priorities in Practice series:

The Essentials of Mathematics, K-6: Effective Curriculum, Instruction, and Assessment by Kathy Checkley (#106032)

The Essentials of Mathematics, Grades 7-12: Effective Curriculum, Instruction, and Assessment by Kathy Checkley (#106129)

The Essentials of Science, Grades K–6: Effective Curriculum, Instruction, and Assessment by Rick Allen (#106206)

For more information: send e-mail to member@ascd.org; call 1-800-933-2723 or 703-578-9600, press 2; send a fax to 703-575-5400; or write to Information Services, ASCD, 1703 N. Beauregard St., Alexandria, VA 22311-1714 USA.